SPEED, STYLE, AND BEAUTY

CARS FROM THE RALPH LAUREN COLLECTION

SPEED, STYLE, AND BEAUTY

MFA PUBLICATIONS

a division of the

Museum of Fine Arts,

Boston

CARS FROM THE RALPH LAUREN COLLECTION

Texts by Beverly Rae Kimes & Winston S. Goodfellow

with photographs by Michael Furman

and an introductory interview with Ralph Lauren

CONTENTS

The Cars

by Beverly Rae Kimes & Winston S. Goodfellow

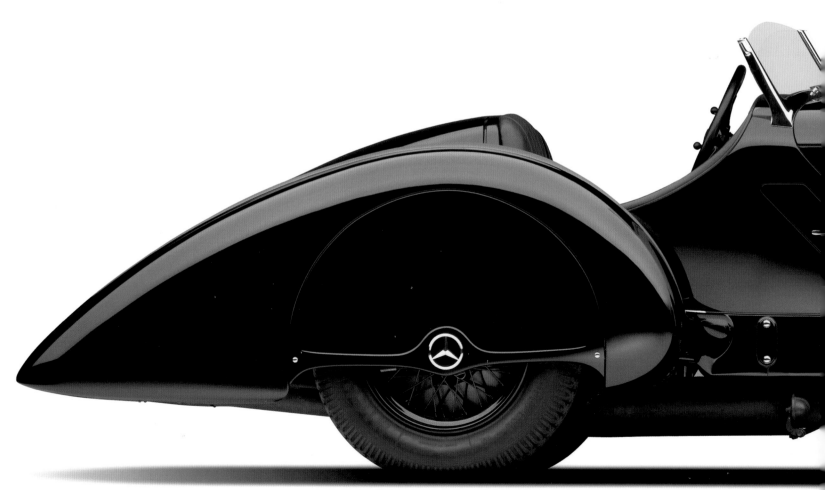

DIRECTOR'S FOREWORD

THE COLLECTIONS of the Museum of Fine Arts, Boston, are among the most diverse of any such institution, and contain many surprises. However, objects used for transportation have never formed a part of our holdings, though there can be no denying that within the field of industrial design, vehicles of every sort have been a source of inspiration for some of the most original stylists of the twentieth century. It is with great excitement, then, that we present the MFA's first exhibition devoted to automobiles.

When we thought of an exhibition about cars, we spoke with several noted experts in the field, including specialists in car restoration, design, and history. They all pointed to Ralph Lauren's magnificent collection as being one of the best, and as one with a unique perspective. It has been a privilege to collaborate with Mr. Lauren on this project, and to be able to share his most celebrated cars with the larger public in the setting of an art museum. Many of the individual pieces in his collection are of the greatest quality, rarity, and beauty. As a group they also provide fascinating insight into the aesthetic sensibilities of one of America's most influential creators of style.

Exhibitions presenting the design of decorative arts and utilitarian objects, including ones that address various modes of modern transportation, have become increasingly popular in recent times. In an effort to reach and inform its broadening audience, the MFA continues to explore and embrace such non-traditional areas of the artistic experience. We thank the exhibition's sponsor, Merrill Lynch, for aiding us in presenting these gorgeous machines to our many visitors. The spectacular sports, racing, and touring cars from the Ralph Lauren collection are sure to arouse envy and nostalgia for automotive enthusiasts, and to be a revelation to those who may never have considered just how glorious a set of four wheels can be.

MALCOLM ROGERS
Ann and Graham Gund Director
Museum of Fine Arts, Boston

PREFACE

by Darcy Kuronen

AS WE MOVE FORWARD in this new millennium, art museums are thoughtfully re-examining the role they play in society. Whatever paths actually present themselves over the coming years, institutions such as the Museum of Fine Arts must surely continue to explore the fundamental and difficult question, "What is art?" that critics, scholars, and devotees will no doubt debate for as long as humans embrace the creative process. Deriving a definitive answer is, ultimately, less important than the vigorous dialogue provoked by posing the question in the first place.

In the preceding century, technology played a more significant role in aesthetic endeavors than during any previous time in history. It affected not only the availability and use of new materials such as plastics and metal alloys, but also the ways in which they could be manipulated to produce desired effects. Likewise, the increasing industrialization enabled by new technologies made the world a much different place, as we moved from a slower-paced agrarian society to one in which speed and productivity were more easily realized and more highly valued.

Perhaps more than any other technological artifact of modern times, it is the automobile that has dramatically changed the way we live. It has dictated our daily rhythms, the layout of our homes, businesses, and cities, and our very sociological structure. A container that has the ability to transport us both physically and psychically, it is a room on wheels that has become an overt and potent emblem of contemporary living. Cars may seem too much a part of our daily existence (in both good and bad ways) to stop and consider their potential as artistic expressions, but like any art form, car design has always reflected ongoing changes in fashion, technology, and societal attitudes.

For decades the world's major car companies have expended considerable effort sketching, developing, rejecting, and ultimately manufacturing automobiles that they have hoped would more perfectly realize one of the most intricate relationships of form and function, and of man and machine. The majority of cars that have rolled off of assembly lines since the early 1900s do not rise to the level of fine art, but there have concurrently been some truly inspired models produced by relatively small firms. Often made in limited numbers of fifty examples or fewer, these cars were commonly created under the guidance of one visionary designer, such as Jean Bugatti, Enzo Ferrari, or Ferdinand Porsche. The chassis of such cars were manufactured to a more-or-less standard form, but there the uniformity ended. Customers could engage their choice of coachbuilder to "body" the car, working to patterns offered by the company or incorporating ideas provided by the client. Not unlike the world of fine art, wealthy patrons were an important part of this equation, enabling car makers to realize striking designs that might have been impractical for mass production. Even so, larger car companies sometimes took inspiration from these handcrafted creations and included elements from them in their own factory models.

Many of the important coachbuilding firms

of Europe transferred their skills for creating a carriage drawn by horses to one powered by an internal combustion engine. The framework of many vehicles predating World War II was made of wood, which was then sheathed with metal panels. This process gradually evolved into one using a metal skeleton (creating a much lighter car overall), but there was still a great deal of artistry involved in shaping and applying the overlying metal skin. In the finest examples, the result is no less impressive than a work from the hands of a brilliant sculptor.

The basic shape and body styling of a great car always attracts our attention first, but a wealth of visual interest can be found in supporting components as well, as is so clearly shown in this book's many close-up photographs. The wheels, grilles, bumpers, headlights, and even gas caps and door handles are minor masterpieces of design in their own right. Likewise, the interiors are frequently rich in artistic detail, with tastefully upholstered seats and an array of knobs, gauges,

and controls on the dashboard. Exotic woods, choice leathers and fabrics, polished metals, and even etched glass all contribute to a stimulating environment from which to operate the car. The engine and drive train, whose physical task is to move the car as speedily and efficiently as possible, are visual marvels of the engineer's art, from the purposeful layout of the cylinders, valves, and exhaust pipes, to the sometimes bewildering arrangement of their attendant parts. It is almost a pity that this delightful machinery is usually hidden from view.

Regardless of one's stance about whether cars are art, the most celebrated examples definitely have a visceral appeal. Park a rare and stylish sports car almost anywhere and you'll soon draw a crowd of vocal admirers that will include both genders, all ages, and a broad range of experiences with owning or operating a car. You needn't have ever sat behind the wheel of a car to be enraptured by one. This is especially true of children, who invariably display a highly animated response toward spectacular cars. But a car's attraction goes far beyond the sensuous lines of its body, some snazzy trim, or the intense growl of a finely tuned motor being revved up. A fine car represents status, freedom, power, celebrity, and a lot more. The narcissistic gratification of being seen driving a great automobile is not to be underestimated.

Although not conceived as art exhibitions per se, the first large events to celebrate beautiful automotive design were outdoor gatherings in Italy and France in the 1920s and '30s called *concours d'élégance*. These affairs provided a venue for display of the latest in automotive style and innovation, accompanied by the latest in clothing fashion. They spread to other parts of Europe, and after temporary disruption during the war they were eventually revived both abroad and in the United States, although they are now competitions and showcases for vintage automobiles rather than contemporary products.

New York's Museum of Modern Art was the first American institution to validate the car as an art form and bring it indoors. In the autumn of 1951 it mounted an exhibition entitled simply "Eight Automobiles," featuring an eclectic mix of vehicles from a sensuous 1939 French Talbot teardrop coupe to a boxy Willys Jeep made in 1951. In the foreword to a booklet that accompanied the exhibition, MOMA's curator of architecture, Arthur Drexler, boldly characterized cars as "hollow, rolling sculpture." Over the years, MOMA has continued to periodically feature cars in their exhibitions, but other art museums have likewise produced shows devoted to automotive design, especially in recent times. These include a large exhibition at the Montreal Museum of Fine Arts in 1995, entitled "Moving Beauty," and a more modest one at the Chrysler Museum in 2003, "La Bella Macchina," devoted entirely to Ferraris. And although the subject was transportation with two wheels rather than four, few were unaware of the wildly successful "Art of the Motorcycle," shown at the Guggenheim Museum in 1998, and subsequently at several other venues.

In mounting its first car exhibition, the MFA is excited to work with leading fashion designer Ralph Lauren. Although Mr. Lauren's car collection is not the largest by any measure, it is highly regarded for the exceptional rarity and caliber of the pieces it contains. Rather than creating a car collection in a systematic way, Mr. Lauren has taken a more individual approach, acquiring particular cars that appeal to his personal sense of aesthetics, much as would any other private collector of fine art. Consequently, the shape and contents of his collection are very much the result of his own keen perception of style and form. Numerous books and articles have been published that present lists of what are considered the most beautiful, most important, or just plain coolest cars of all time. Suffice it to say that a great many of the car models in the Lauren collection consistently appear in these surveys.

In spite of the individual character of the Lauren collection, there is an overall unity to its makeup. With the exception of certain utilitarian vehicles, such as vintage jeeps, pickups, and a nostalgic Ford "Woody" station wagon, all of his cars are European, and all were created for racing or touring. In his own words, it is their "functional beauty" that appeals to him. He is not attracted to cars that are dazzling just for the sake of being dazzling, but rather to ones on which the lines, curves, vents, and fittings serve a particular purpose. That purpose is most often speed, so it is little wonder that a number of the cars from the Lauren collection have a racing pedigree, even if they were also intended for use on the open road.

It is hard to predict what our modes of personal transportation will be by the end of this century, let alone how they will be fueled. But it is almost certain that we will continue to value vehicles that appeal to our sense of speed, style, and beauty. Will the sleek, sensual lines of a 1958 Ferrari Testarossa someday seem as quaint as a Ford Model T? Or are such cars timeless in their form, like other great works of three-dimensional art? Only time will tell. For now, it is fascinating to reflect on and admire some of the finest automotive design of the past century.

AN INTERVIEW WITH RALPH LAUREN

by Darcy Kuronen

Ralph Lauren launched the Polo brand in 1968 with a man's tie and a singular point of view about style, elegance, and quality. From original design in luxury apparel, accessories, and home décor, Mr. Lauren has built a company with products sold in sixty-five countries. The Polo Ralph Lauren Company is recognized today as one of the world's leading and most innovative design houses, and arguably the most influential.

The following interview took place in May 2004 in Mr. Lauren's corporate offices. As with his designs, Ralph Lauren seeks sophistication and exceptional taste in the many magnificent cars he owns, and his remarks about them, not surprisingly, address their aura and presence as much as their performance.

What was the first automobile that you remember as a child, and why do you remember it?

I'm not sure it could be called a real car, but I remember looking out the window of my apartment house when I was about five or six years old. There were these twins about my age, two boys, and they had just gotten a bright red fire engine for their birthday, with two bells on the back. I always wanted a car like that. It was big enough to get inside instead of just wheeling it on the floor. I thought, I can get into this car like it was a real thing, a fire truck, a bright red fire truck. So I guess the first car I ever fell in love with was this toy car, and I never forgot it.

Were you a car enthusiast from childhood?

When I was growing up, cars were somehow part of every boy's life. You weren't aware of being an enthusiast, you were just tuned in. I remember sitting with my friends, and we'd count the cars; we'd say how many Chevrolets had gone by, how many Oldsmobiles, how many Pontiacs. You could recognize every car.

Given that you grew up in New York City, was there a family car? On what car did you learn to drive?

[*Laughing*] I learned to drive in my father's navy blue Pontiac fastback sedan, with the torpedo back that went straight down. It was a beautiful car, and it had an Indian head on the front hood that was a golden color. I loved that car. The only thing is that I was the youngest in a family of four, so by the time I got the car it was pretty old and shabby. And then I still had to battle my two other brothers to be able to take a date out in it. I had to drive about an hour to pick up my girlfriend in Brooklyn. So somewhere between battling my brothers for the use of the car, and the fact that it was such an old car, it whetted my appetite to have something special someday.

Was there a single car that made you look upon the automobile as more than a means to get from here to there?

For me, a car was always something special. It brought you somewhere else—the car was a way of entering another environment. Eating in the car, driving to the country, stopping at a restaurant, being on your way to somewhere —the car was part of my culture growing up, and as a young boy I never quite saw it as a status symbol so much as an escape, or an entry into wonderful worlds.

What was the first great, interesting, or collector car that you purchased?

Ralph Lauren with his dog Rugby seated in his 1957 Jaguar XKSS, Bedford, New York, 1998.

The first car I ever bought on my own savings was a 1961 Morgan. It was all white with red leather seats. It had a strap on the hood and the body construction was traditional '30s, which gave it a very rugged, utility look at a time when you very rarely saw something like a Jeep, for instance. To me, the Morgan was a great car that should never have its top up—true Morgan owners would never put the top up. They would go top-down in the coldest weather. What's so appealing about this car is the sport of driving it and its ruggedness. Sort of like backpackers today, or the early four-wheel drivers, in that they'd put all their utility gear inside and take a ride somewhere in the middle of winter with the top down. So I entered the Morgan club as one of those guys, because that's how I saw myself.

Do you still own it?

I don't have that Morgan anymore. I had it when I got married, but I had to choose between that car and my wife, because we wanted to get an apartment and I couldn't afford a garage in Manhattan. I was also concerned that if the car broke down I wouldn't have the money to fix it. So I sold it to a friend of mine in Massachusetts. I went to this beautiful area where he lived and I left it with him, and then I rode the bus for about three hours to get back home. Looking back on it, I think I gave up that Morgan a little too early. I wasn't ready. So the first car I bought after I could afford a car again was another Morgan, a 1966 four-seater, which I still own today.

Do you have a favorite car in your current collection, either in terms of visual beauty or in terms of how it drives?

Cars are like children; it's very hard to say that any one is my favorite. There are little things about each car that you come to love, whether it's the look, the steering wheel, the wire wheels, the way it drives, or even the way it drives differently when you put the top up. They all have identities; they all have spirits and characteristics that are really endearing in some way. That's why I never like to sell my cars, and I've always accumulated more cars. I would not want to part with the ones I have.

Some of them might not be as fast as others, or as racy, or as shiny, but each one has a distinct character of its own.

As time went on, each car came to represent a different part of my life. After I started my company, for example, I bought a 1971 Mercedes 3.5 convertible. It was the last hand built convertible they made. I was telling my son the other day that I was exactly his age when I bought that car. Here we were sitting in this car, driving along, and I was looking at my oldest son, who is now thirty-two, the same age I had been. That car has history, memories. It is more beautiful today than ever before, and I will never sell it.

What is it about a given automobile that makes you feel you have to have it?

As I started to buy cars, I didn't know I was building a collection. I just wanted the cars I was dreaming about. Once you drive a good one, it's like having a fever.

My first major car purchase was a Porsche Turbo that I bought in 1978. I went through years of renting cars and putting my kids in the back seat or the front seat or wherever I could put them. Having three kids always made it a little crowded. Anyway, my first legitimate speed car that had some real technology to it was this 1979 Porsche Turbo. It was really fast, and it was a very important time for the Porsche company, the beginning of turbos. After buying that one, I became very, very excited about cars.

I drove other cars as well, and then at one point a friend of mine said, "I'd like you to drive my Ferrari." I said, "Well, I really don't like Ferraris," but I climbed inside and I absolutely fell in love with that car. I got hooked on the Ferrari after driving it only once. Somewhere along the line I bought myself a Daytona Spyder, which is an amazing car. And that was the beginning of my Ferrari fever.

Tell me about the experience of driving older collectable cars.

They are all different. They have different sounds, they have different feels. There's a different feeling to the clutch. There's a different power. It's interesting, but you can drive a car one day and it will have a certain feel, and

Ricky and Ralph Lauren in their Porsche at Lime Rock racetrack, Connecticut, 1977.

which cars we like better and why. Sometimes we'll test the same cars twice, and the results will be different each time.

What kind of driver are you? Do you like to put your cars through their paces?

I can't evaluate what kind of driver I am. I thought at one time that I'd be a race car driver, that I'd replace Paul Newman, but when I went to racing school I found that I wasn't as good as I'd thought. In fact, the first time I spun out, I wanted to quit—it was a little shocking. But I stayed with it. And the driving fever never quite went away. I don't like just going around and around doing laps—I really prefer driving on the road. I like the feeling of being in the open air, with the trees and the country surrounding me, driving somewhere, feeling the car and the power it has, its spirit—that is part of my sensibility, not racing around a track.

Does your family take any part in the creation or use of your car collection?

Everyone in my family enjoys the cars. My wife does not necessarily care to drive them herself, but she's really the one who pushes me to take drives, and she loves the cars. So for her as well there's a spirit of relaxation, and pleasure. I always ask her questions when I'm driving: How do you like this car? How does this feel? Do you like that sound? She's a very good critic.

What made you decide to exhibit your cars in an art museum? Do you view great cars as art?

I've always seen cars as art. Moving art. While friends of mine were into paintings, I somehow felt that the real beauty of owning a rare and magnificently designed car was the fact that you can use it. You can look at it, enjoy its visual qualities, as with a painting, but you can also get inside and drive it—which means both enjoying the drive itself and going somewhere with it. How these cars are put together, the purposefulness with which they were created, in every detail—the engine, the mechanics, the outside ornamentation, the design of the wheels, the whole spirit—is very, very exciting. And on top of that you have the men who created these cars, Mr. Porsche, Mr. Bugatti, Mr. Ferrari, and their backgrounds,

you drive the same car the next day and it won't feel the same. These cars have moods that change with the weather, or with the driver's own moods. I can drive a certain car one day with great pleasure, and the next day I'll be disappointed that the experience isn't as good as the day before.

Do you notice particular distinctions in the way each of them rides and handles, or the sounds their engines make?

The sounds of cars are very distinctive. You can hear if one of the cylinders is fouled up or if the car isn't running right. You become attuned to the feel, the power, and the sound, because they all work together in an orchestrated way. Porsches, Ferraris, and Jaguars are all different, and the sounds they make are different, the shifting is different, the spirit of driving is totally different—yet they're all enjoyable, which is what makes it so exciting. When you own a few cars, you can have your own tests. I have my own road and track, so I do comparison drives with my family to see

The RLX running shoe, introduced in 1999.

Opposite:
The Ralph Lauren RL-CF1 Carbon Fiber Chair, introduced in 2003 and inspired by his McLaren F1.

Below:
Polo by Ralph Lauren Luggage, introduced in 1979 and inspired by a black Porsche.

their heritages, their fascinating histories, their reasons for driving and building these cars—I find it all very stimulating.

Many of your cars are hand built affairs from a time when craftsmen were able to lavish considerable attention to every detail. Is this one of the aspects that draws you to these beautiful objects?

Well, I've always loved quality. And I've always loved machines that are the product of someone taking his passion for building and using it to create beautiful shapes or sounds that give pleasure. I love craftsmanship, because handcrafting has always given me a sense of personal connection to the maker. At the same time, whether or not they're handcrafted, I've seen the progress cars have made through the years, and it's amazing where they are today—in their quality of comfort, their speed, the way they are designed, and the way they can now put a small engine into a car and still make it go like a rocket ship.

I've heard you speak of "functional beauty" when referring to cars. What do you mean by this expression?

I've always liked purposeful things, things that are designed not just to be decorative. These cars were designed by creators who had a point of view, a mission. Their aim was not only to make the car look good, but also to make it go faster, or to improve its comfort. The cars I've most enjoyed are the ones that were hand built, limited in production, and that had a sense of purpose. Most of them were created for the track—they were built for speed, they were built to win the race—and that leads to something very exciting. When you're building something to win a race, and at the same time you fit it with amazing wheels and hubcaps, a gorgeous steering wheel and a rakish windshield, you turn out something that is both a work of beauty and highly functional.

I understand that cars have had a considerable influence on some of your own designs. Could you tell me something about that?

As a fashion designer, I'm always searching for ideas. And my ideas come from my life, they come from my work, they come from everyday living. Cars have always had some im-

pact, because today cars are designed and sold in many different ways to stimulate different passions or different senses. I look at a car and I look at a hubcap or a gas cap, or at the carbon fiber that's being used today to make cars lighter and stronger, and something about it might inspire me to adapt the idea for one of my products. I might think that a certain car seat is comfortable, and I love the way it looks—why not do this in my furniture collection? There was one car that excited me when I was designing running shoes. Running shoes and automobiles are not as far apart as you might think. Both are ever-changing, they move with the trends, they are constantly being redesigned. Cars pick up ideas from the fashion industry, and the fashion industry picks up ideas from the automotive world or from whatever environments we are looking at. So there is an interchange.

If you love cars—their upholstery, their ornaments, their wooden steering wheels, and different shapes—as a designer you can't help being stimulated. I have been inspired by various cars to create many different things—luggage, for example. When I wanted to put luggage in my black Porsche, I thought to myself, I can't put tan leather in this black Darth Vader car. I need something black, and I need something with utility that represents what this car is. So I designed luggage with a utility exterior and with the glove leather inside, which represented my feelings about Porsche at that time. In some ways the Porsche was somewhat ugly, compared with a Bentley or one of the great old cars from the twenties and thirties, but it was also a very purposeful, functional vehicle. The luggage I designed had that same feel to it—black, techie, utilitarian luggage to put inside this black, utilitarian car. Most recently, my McLaren inspired the creation of our carbon fiber chair, the RL-CF1. It is an amazing technological and design feat using fifty-four layers of tissue carbon once only found in high-performance jets and race cars.

In Europe during the 1920s and '30s, the latest in automotive and clothing fashions were shown together at events called *concours d'élégance.*

What is it about these two products that you think made them a good pairing?

Automobiles are an expression of the individual who buys or drives them. We represent ourselves with our cars, just as we represent ourselves with the clothes we wear. The automobile has become an accessory to our lives— a functional accessory, but an accessory nonetheless. When you see a guy driving an all-black car, he looks cool and sexy, but if you then saw the same guy in a light blue convertible, he would somehow look a little softer. It's not quite the same. A car is an extension of one's personal taste, of one's style and image. When people go to special events to show their cars and their clothes, it's all part of the same set. The clothes we wore in the thirties and forties went with the kinds of cars we drove. Even now, a woman who thinks of herself as wearing a long evening gown, going out for dinner, or attending a gala event would imagine herself in a shiny black limousine or a beautiful luxury car, as opposed to the sports car she might drive by day. So cars are more than a conveyance to get to from one place to another. They are a key part of our taste and its expression.

People speak of the womanly curves found in certain cars, and of course these same vehicles are often collected and driven primarily by men. Any thoughts on this?

I have never connected the design of cars with shapes of people or their sexuality. There is certainly an undeniable power to a race car —it is a sexy machine.

Some of your cars have been featured in ads for your products. Tell me a bit about the thinking behind this.

Well, again, the cars are part of the environment, they're part of your statement about your style. When you buy furniture, say, or a house, you are aiming for a certain look. If you envision an elegant stone country house, you don't think of a Jeep. You think of something more like a Jaguar, a dark green Jaguar on a country road. Or something equally elegant, with a wood dashboard and a wooden steering wheel. But if you live on the beach, that same car might not be what you want. In that case,

you might want a Jeep with an open top and a sense of utility. Probably the colors would be light—light blue or yellow, or something that reflects the mood of where you are and what you're using it for. If you live on a farm, or you like the ruggedness of the country, you might have a pickup truck, and that would be your sensibility. Having lived in many different places, I can attest that it feels right to drive different cars in those different places. Again, each car in its own way makes a statement about who you are and what your style and your tastes are. Whether it's an old pickup truck or a shiny new sports car, it represents an element of your total style.

Of the cars in your collection, the hairiest is the Blower Bentley. Most of your cars have a certain grace, but the Blower is more of a brute. What attracted you to it?

The Blower is on some levels an agricultural car. Mr. Bugatti likened it to a truck, but it goes 110 miles an hour. There are louvers and straps and guards and light grilles, and a very tough engine in the front. It's a utilitarian, industrial, purposeful car that has a beauty in its ruggedness. And speed.

It's a very heavy car to drive. In the 1920s this might not have been so unusual, but today I find it amazing that this car, which is so heavy and so full of equipment, could also be so fast to drive. I get as much of a thrill driving a Bentley as I do driving a Porsche.

One of your most recent acquisitions is the Alfa Romeo 8C 2900 Mille Miglia. It has been described by some as the finest pre-World War II sports car, and also one of the greatest automobiles of all time. Do you agree?

I don't know that I can answer you as completely as I'd like because I don't have access to the car yet—it's being restored. The Mille Miglia is indeed one of the great cars in automotive history, in that its engineering was way ahead of its time. It was built in the thirties, but it feels more like a car of the fifties or sixties. It's very light to drive, and it feels very efficient.

The Bugatti Type 59 racer is an odd fit in your collection, since there's really nothing else like

Ralph Lauren with his Bugatti Type 57SC Atlantic Coupe, "Best of Show" at the Pebble Beach Concours d'Elégance, 1991.

it among the other cars. The French racing champion René Dreyfus, who drove for the Bugatti team in the early thirties, hated the Type 59. What's your attraction to this car?

The Type 59 may not have won many races, and it was obsolete when it was introduced, but it was a car that was designed totally from an aesthetic point of view—a race car that was a work of art. Every Bugatti is in a certain way an art object, from its dashboard to its tooling to its engine. And if you pick up the hood, you will notice the way it's finished. Every detail on the car is like fine art, or maybe I should say like a very fine watch. It's refined, it's elegant, it's fast, and it is also very beautiful.

Reactions to the Bugatti Atlantic seem to be either black or white, never gray. The car either knocks your socks off or it doesn't. What do you think about it?

As far as I'm concerned, the Atlantic is probably the most beautiful car in the world in both its details and its overall shape, which was totally original. To me, the Atlantic is very, very distinctive, from its crafted dashboard to its interior to its overall refinement, not to mention its speed for that time. You can view this car from any angle and it still looks amazing.

One of the criteria for beautiful design is that it never looks dated. The cars that I've collected through the years look as good today as they did at the time they were made. They don't look like old, outdated cars. They look like something that makes you think, Wow, where can I get that now? That's been my guiding principle for automobiles and the way I've collected them. It also has guided my sense of design, in that I've never designed for obsolescence—I've designed for longevity. Good design is about staying power as well as about being current. The Bugattis, especially, were designed for beauty and elegance and timelessness.

It seems like the three fantastic Bugattis you own present a more powerful message as a group than they might separately. Do you agree?

The way I saw them, they fulfilled my dream of what a car should look like, in that they have wonderful details. Each one—the Type 59 racer, the 57SC Atlantic coupe, and the 57SC Gangloff convertible—is unique. But as a group they share the most beautiful Bugatti design elements in terms of their shape, their lowness to the ground, their details, their engineering, and there are no other cars that look like them. They are ageless.

Your Mercedes SSK is the personal design statement of its original owner, Count Carlo Felice Trossi, but the SSK is also one of the most coveted automobiles in the world. Which of these two factors persuaded you most forcefully to acquire this car?

I remember going to Pebble Beach with my family and seeing this car drive down and I was mesmerized. And later, when I had an opportunity to drive the car and ultimately buy it, it was quite an exciting moment. I have never bought cars just because they are rare. They have all represented some sort of beauty to me. This is a one-off sports car designed by a man who was very influential in the racing world— and he had a wonderful taste level. I think he designed this car because he was a race car driver, but he wanted individuality in his road going sports car. On some level, what he did is what I would have done had I been a race car driver and lived in a time when you could create your own cars. He put his personal stamp on it, and the result is that it's a beautiful piece, one of a kind. It looks like an amazing 1930s car, but also, especially from the back, it could be the Batmobile from today's movies.

Postwar cars from Mercedes-Benz are better known for their engineering than for their style. What drew you to the 300SLs?

Although Mercedes has always been known for its engineering, the 300SL is another example of a car with a distinctive shape, especially in the "gullwing" doors that open upward. As I saw it, the car could boast speed and an important racing heritage, but it also had that other

requirement of mine: beauty that grew out of its purposefulness. Both the SL convertible and the Gullwing were unique cars that, again, have that timeless beauty. Whenever I drive the SL, it never ceases to turn heads. Even young people who have never seen one of these before ask where they can get one. It has a beauty all its own, and, like the Bugattis, no age.

The Jaguar XK120 is considered one of the most memorable sports cars of the modern era. Why do you think that's so?

All the Jaguars represent to my mind both the English countryside and the English race tracks. They look great in that wonderful dark British racing green color. Some were beautiful in shape and functional on the track. The D-type in particular was one of my favorites because it won Le Mans a few times, but also because of its timeless shape and sleek design. The fin on the back of the D-type is quite amazing. It looks like a car from outer space, but it was built in the 1950s.

All the Jaguars you own are very distinguished models, but some might wonder why you don't have an E-type from the 1960s. Have you intentionally avoided acquiring this model?

You never know why certain cars don't hit you. The E-type was a great car, the most famous and most commercial of the Jaguars, but somehow the D-type always impressed me as the original, the race car with the original shape. Its distinctive design was the forerunner of the E-type. I guess the simplest way to say it is that the D-type was the model that responded to my sensibilities when it came to Jaguars.

"Excellence Was Expected" was the subtitle of Karl Ludvigsen's landmark history of the Porsche. Its pedigree is exemplary, and Porsche people are a breed onto themselves. Do you think of yourself as a Porsche person?

When I was growing up, or at least when I got to the point of deciding what cars I wanted, there was an image of the Porsche as the more intelligent car, as opposed to the Ferrari, which was the racier car. Though Porsches and Ferraris are both amazing products, there was a division between them. I've always loved Porsches, and I've always loved Ferraris, so it's hard to decide between them. When I drive the Ferraris, they have a sound and a scream to them, and a sexiness, that is very different from the Porsches. Porsches suggest an industrial sensibility. I truly enjoy that industrial quality, the tightness and efficiency, just as much as I enjoy the qualities of the Ferrari. Through the 959s, I've loved the Porsches as well as I've loved any car. The other day I was in the rain, and I was driving a Porsche, coming home from the movies. It felt so good to be in this efficient, safe car that you knew was going to get you where you wanted to go, that had a kind of coziness about it.

Ferraris make up a large percentage of your collection. Do you have a particular fondness for this make?

When I think of Ferraris, I think of the color red. And I think of Italy because the Italian race cars are generally red. The Ferraris are fast, they make amazing sounds, they are designed with the flair of Italy, and they all have purposefulness. In the early days, when Ferraris were raced, they were simply fast. They

Ralph Lauren's 1955 Mercedes-Benz 300SL Gullwing Coupe.

were designed to win. But it's in their accidental beauty that I would define what Ferrari are. They were made by Enzo Ferrari and his team to win the next race, and that was their entire goal. But along the way, in building these purposeful vehicles, they created a kind of beauty that a schooled designer probably could not re-create today. The emotion and passion Italians have for their cars came through in their body designs.

Is it hard to imagine a Ferrari in any other color than red?

You know, I don't like red cars. But Ferrari have to be red.

If you could keep only one of your Ferraris, which would it be?

Again, I'd have to sell all my cars at once in order to get rid of any of them. It would be very hard if someone asked me to pick out my favorite cars. I think I'd have to decide not to drive cars anymore, and just close the door. The GTO Ferrari, built in 1962–63, is considered by many to be the great Ferrari collector's piece and the ultimate car in its class. But I have many different ultimates that I think are the most beautiful for the different years in which they were created. The Testa Rossa, for example, is an amazing car. But all of them have their different spirits.

Do you admire the McLaren F1 more for its looks or the way it drives?

The McLaren is like no other car I've driven in my life. The first time I saw a McLaren was in a London showroom. The display was a black cave, and here was this silver piece of art. My first thought was, well, that's unusual, but what else does it do? But as I read up on it, and as I took test drives in it, I realized that this was a car like none other. It was like piloting a rocket ship. The McLaren was built as the ultimate driving car—a road car, not a race car, but later transposed into a race car. It's built in carbon fiber and has three seats across the front, with the driver sitting in the middle. The experience of driving this car is truly unique. Although it was built in 1996, the car still holds the top speed record for a production car of 240 miles an hour, and can go from 0 to 60 in about 3.2 seconds. So it has beauty, it has art, it has racing magic, and it fills all the criteria that one could ever dream of in a car. Plus, you can also drive it to go get groceries.

Have you ever tested the authenticity of the speedometer?

I haven't had it near 240 miles an hour, if that's what you mean. I've pushed it up fairly high, but it was still about 100 miles an hour below that, and even that felt fast enough. Part of me would like to know what it feels like to go 240 miles an hour. The McLaren Company does have a spot where they safely show you what it feels like. But even at 140 miles an hour, or 100 miles an hour, even though you know you're going very fast, it feels like you're only going 50. It's a unique piece of art and automotive design.

The vast majority of your collection is European and sporty, but the two cars at the end of this book are not. The Ford "Woody" station wagon is almost as proverbially American as apple pie. Was that a factor in your acquiring one, or is this mainly a working car for you?

Well, again, it's about my sense of my own life, how I live and what I love. I love sport and I like speed, and I love design, and I also love the spirit of living in the country. And I think the Woody captures this spirit. It's also about the dream of the automobile. When I was growing up and reading books in school, the characters were all called Jim and Judy or something like that, and the station wagon was the car of comfort for the family. The family would go for a ride, mother and father and sister and brother and their little dog. It was the ideal life

of the American culture. That dark green Woody represented something to me. It was not a ritzy car; it was a car that the family could afford. It represented part of the dream of my life that had to do with the culture I grew up in.

Regarding the 1951 Willys Jeep, was this strictly a utilitarian purchase, or were you motivated by its unabashedly spartan look, or its history, or maybe even a Bill Mauldin cartoon?

It's about the essence of utility. The Jeep is a tin can that can go through water—that can go through anything. It's the original four-wheel-drive outing vehicle. You can climb mountains in a Jeep, go over rocks, go practically anywhere. It's a utility vehicle with a distinctly outdoorsy spirit. In its own way, it represents a kind of functional beauty.

Do you think the great age of automotive design is now behind us, or do you think car designers are still capable of creating products whose artistry will stand the test of time?

We seem to be witnessing a return to individuality in automobiles. When I started collecting, it was because the cars I saw were all mass-produced. Somewhere around the 1970s cars became indistinguishable. In most cases, they still are today, because there are so many cars out there. Carmakers are recognizing that the car is part of our culture, and that the driver sees it as an extension of his or her personality. I think that some of the designers today are very, very good. I'm seeing new shapes, new designs, and new technology that all have really lifted the contemporary automobile to a new level, and that make it once more an extension of taste.

Ralph Lauren behind the wheel of his 1930 Mercedes-Benz "Count Trossi" SSK, Bedford, New York, 1996.

1929 BLOWER BENTLEY

SOME CARS attain mythic status in spite of themselves. Although famously unsuccessful, the Blower Bentley was arguably the most glamorous and thrilling of all Bentleys ever built. Its supercharger, or "blower," was larger than many automobile engines of the day and loomed menacingly in front of the radiator. The sheer audacity of the Blower Bentley was breathtaking; its sight and sound virtually precluded its ever being forgotten. Walter Owen Bentley did not make automobiles for the meek. Still, he hated this one, for W. O., as everyone knew him, counted the Blower among the several factors that caused him to lose his company to Rolls-Royce in 1931.

Bentley's life as an automaker had begun shortly after the Armistice ending World War I. His previous business—importing the French D.F.P. automobile in partnership with his brother—had not made him rich, and he had to take out a mortgage to build his car factory at Cricklewood, an inner suburb of London. Anxious to get on with the project, W. O. announced the first Bentley before one had been built, indeed several months before Bentley

Frank Clement, W. O. Bentley, and John Duff (left to right) with the 1924 Le Mans–winning 3-liter Bentley.

Motors Ltd. itself was formally organized. Capital stock was £200,000; cash in the bank was less than 10 percent of that. W. O.'s company would teeter on the brink of financial ruin for many of its dozen years of life.

But if fortune was never consistent, fame was quick to arrive and stayed to the end thanks to racing. W. O. said he engaged in competition to enhance his business. His first win was in May 1921, four months before the first production car was delivered to a customer. By the mid-twenties Bentley Motors had begun its domination of the Twenty-Four Hours of Le Mans, which would eventually award the marque five victories in seven years and fix W. O.'s Bentley forever in the national consciousness as the archetypical British sports car.

As thundering as the cars were, their mystique emanated as well from the men who raced them: the storied Bentley Boys, a gaggle of rich Brits who drove and played together very well.

J.D. Benjafield with a Blower at Pontlieue shortly after throwing a tread during Le Mans 1930.

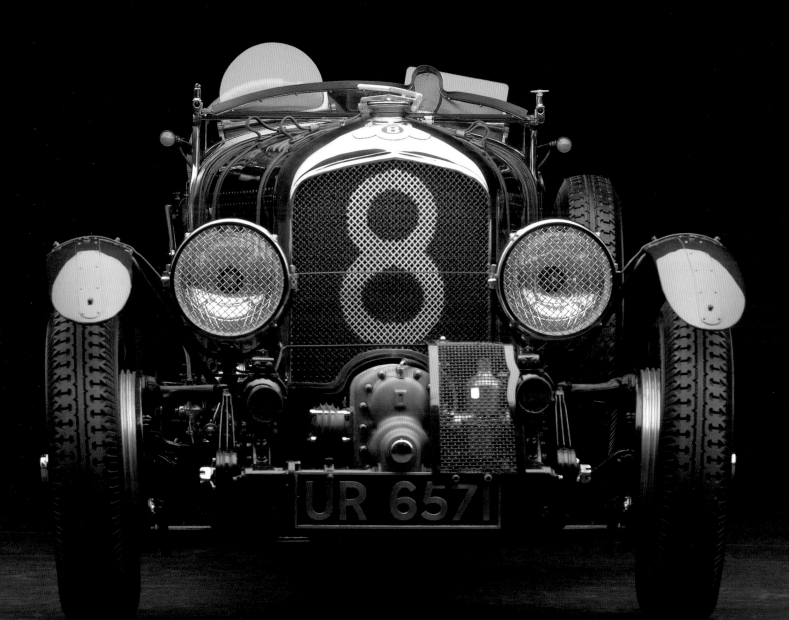

Four of them lived alongside one another on Grosvenor Square in Mayfair. Their dusk-to-dawn parties were the talk of London and provided regular fodder for the tabloids. They skied the Alps, sailed the Mediterranean, and cavorted on the Riviera. As one of their number, Sir Henry "Tim" Birkin, wrote in 1932, "I question if we shall ever see again as cheery a crowd."

It was Birkin who fathered the Blower Bentley. He had won Le Mans in 1928 with a 4½ Litre and was convinced this felicitous situation would not likely recur without some changes. The competition was hard at work developing faster cars to make sure it did not. Birkin approached W. O. with the idea of a blower or supercharger to realize a high-compression, high-revving engine that would increase performance. It was an attractive way to get more from less, and contemporary thought was on Birkin's side. W. O. was aghast. "To supercharge a Bentley engine was to pervert its design and corrupt its performance," he wrote famously in his autobiography. He was strictly old school: you need more power, you build a bigger engine. His first Bentley had been the 3 Litre, which he bumped up to 4½ when competition necessitated. He was now at work on the Speed Six.

Though W. O. was as anxious as Birkin for greater speed and acceleration, he insisted that it not be accomplished "by any falsely induced means." Supercharging would be forced on him, however, because Birkin persuaded his fellow Bentley Boy, Woolf Barnato, that a blower was the answer, and Woolf had become president of the company after bailing W. O. out of one of his financial eddies a while before.

Fifty Blowers had to be produced to meet Le Mans requirements, and Cricklewood would build those. But W. O. was adamant that if Birkin wanted to race the bloody thing, he would have to see to that elsewhere. W. O. wanted the factory to focus on race prep of the Speed Six. Birkin set up his own shop in Welwyn City, purloining Bentley race engineer Clive Gallop to help him. They in turn contacted Charles Amherst Villiers, who knew more about forced induction than anybody else in Great Britain. Villiers designed a supercharger that more than doubled the 4½ Litre's 110 hp to 240.

Instead of installing the blower in the engine compartment, making its presence known by a comely display of pipes on the side of the body, as in the Mercedes-Benz SSK, Birkin and his cohorts chose to mount the blower of the 4½ Litre Supercharged Bentley (as it was properly called) on the crankshaft in front of a modified radiator, where it glowered menacingly between the dumb irons for all the world to see.

Paperwork was filed for participation at Le Mans in mid-June 1929 but the entry had to be scratched when the car could not be made ready in time. Engine failure put the Blower out of its race debut in the British Automobile Racing Club's Six Hours Race at Brooklands two weeks later. During the next fortnight a second car was completed and the pair of them was raced in the Irish Grand Prix, where they finished third and eighth, which would prove the highlights of the Blower's maiden year. A three-car team was ready for the Tourist Tro-

A Blower Bentley taking the outer banking at 120 mph during the 500 Mile Race at Brooklands, October 1931.

phy in Ireland in August, but the sole Blower left on the circuit at the finish, driven by Birkin with a chagrined W. O. as passenger, was in eleventh place. The season ended in October at the British Racing Drivers Club's 500 Mile Race at Brooklands, where the Blower caught fire.

Meanwhile, Birkin had run out of his own money for this whim. Fortunately he had both charm and connections. The Honorable Dorothy Paget, daughter of a baron and good friend, adored automobiles and cheerfully offered whatever financial support might be necessary to field a team of three cars for the following season, most especially Le Mans.

W. O. arrived in France hoping to repeat his Speed Six Le Mans victory of the year before. As owner of a race team, Paget was ebullient. Birkin was convinced that 1930 was the Blower's year. But trouble began even before the starting flag. The first of the three cars couldn't be made ready. Birkin took the race lap record with a second car at 89.69 mph— and with no tread left remaining on his left rear tire—in a titanic struggle with the lone Mercedes SSK, driven by Rudi Caracciola, but then burned a valve and retired on lap 138. The third Blower, driven by J. Dudley Benjafield, the only medical doctor Bentley Boy, suffered a collapsed piston six laps later.

One of W. O.'s Speed Sixes won, the fourth consecutive Le Mans victory by a Bentley since 1927. At the conclusion of the race, Bentley Motors officially withdrew from further com-

petition to focus on the larger fight to stay alive. How much blame W. O. placed upon the Blower for losing that fight depended upon when you asked him. In his autobiography, he assigned percentages: 70 to the dreadful economy following the stock market crash, 10 to the Blower, the remainder to the production car developed as a last-gap effort for survival. But on another occasion he lamented the "great deal of goodwill" that was lost because "the supercharged cars lacked the steady reliability which had, from the beginning, been part of Bentley Motors' religion." He also complained that the Blowers "added to the slightly suspect 'fast-living' connotations associated with the marque."

At the Tourist Trophy the month following the Bentley withdrawal, all three Blowers started and all three retired with engine failure. Birkin and friends continued racing their own pressurized 4½ Litre Bentleys even after Rolls-Royce acquired the company, following which plans were laid to create a refined sports car out of W. O.'s unabashed brute. Retirements and crashes marked the remainder of the Blower's career. A second in the 1930 French Grand Prix would prove its best finish. That the winning car was a Bugatti half its weight was rather impressive. Equally impressive was Birkin's breaking of the Outer Circuit record at 137.96 mph at Brooklands in 1932. Although records at Brooklands often fell like rain, Birkin's was still his when he died the following year. Still, the Blower's was not a race record that warranted boasting.

One is left with the mystique. The suggestion of the improper, the aspect that hints at the bawdy, resulted in the Blower becoming arguably both the most controversial and the most desired Bentley ever built. That there was something magical about a supercharger in full cry was recognized by even W. O. Bentley. "No one could resist its lure," he said, "and of course they *were* very fast while they lasted."

The Blower Bentley was the automobile Ian Fleming chose for 007 to drive in his early novels—James Bond's first car. Of course.

—BRK

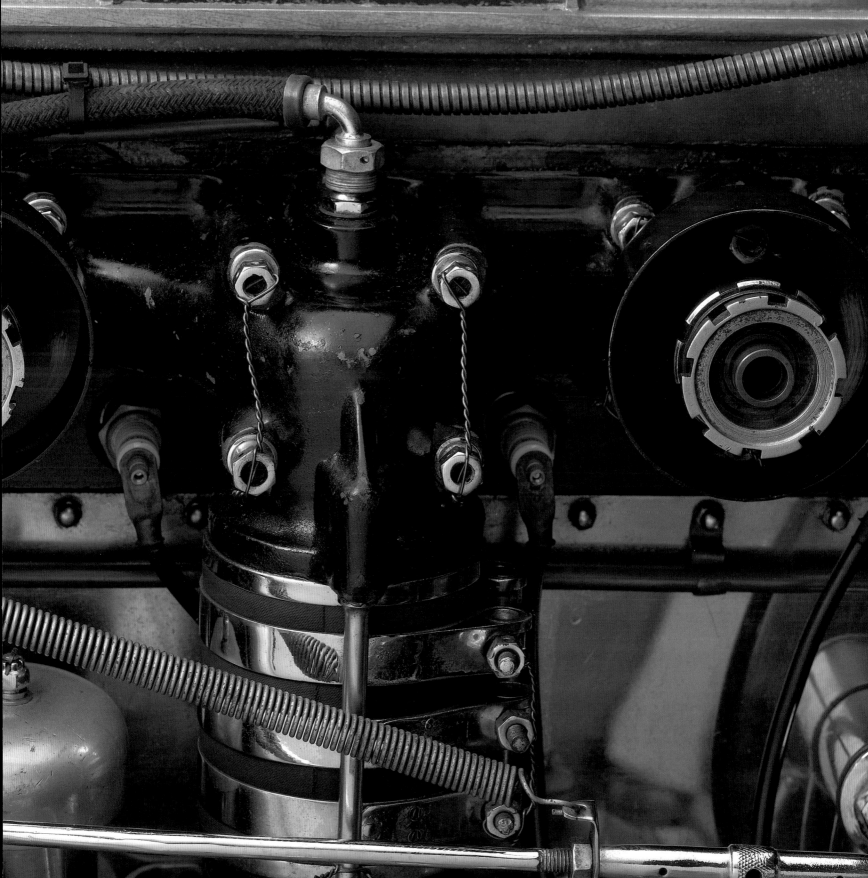

1930 MERCEDES-BENZ "COUNT TROSSI" SSK

THE SSK WAS A METAPHOR for the Roaring Twenties and the apotheosis of a sports car, in addition to being as innovative as Gropius's Bauhaus. Its bold and highly polished radiator grille, the rakish wind screen, the long hood enveloping more than half the body, the three great exhaust pipes emerging from the side, all made the SSK the most widely copied car of its generation.

The consensus is that although the SSK's look could be imitated, its decibel level could not. Whether the sound produced resembled a Valkyrie's cry or an Irish banshee's scream was hotly debated. Whichever, it was music to its owner, terrifying to the uninitiated. With the supercharger engaged, a virtual herd of extra horses was unleashed—which could be tweaked to 300 bhp, an extraordinary figure for the period. Journalists of the day aptly coined "elephant blower" for the device.

The SSK was an evolution of the first series to bear the name Mercedes-Benz following the mid-twenties merger of Germany's two oldest automobile companies: Benz et Cie. and Daimler Motoren-Gesellschaft. The latter's product had been called a Mercedes since the turn of the century when distributor Emil Jellinek chose his daughter's name for the special car built for him by Wilhelm Maybach. Jellinek took the car to Nice Week where it overwhelmed the competition, winning the

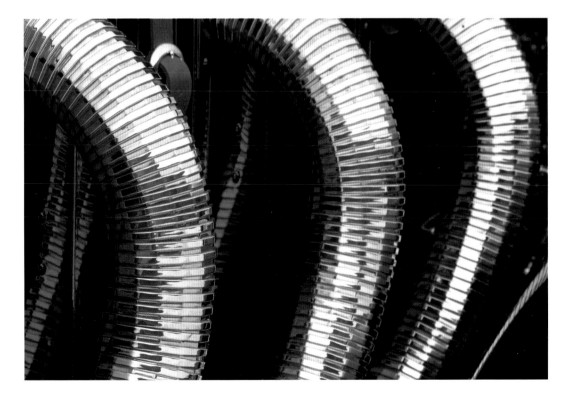

distance race, the sprint, and the hill climb. Racing to victory became a favored pastime for the Mercedes thereafter.

To keep that happening following the merger, Wilhelm Kissel, the Benz man who now headed Daimler-Benz Aktiengesellschaft, directed chief engineer Dr. Ferdinand Porsche to come up with a new winner. Porsche had joined the company in the early twenties shortly after throwing a cigarette lighter at a board member and storming out of Austro-Daimler in Vienna. He had a fearsome temper but was prodigiously talented. Porsche refashioned the pre-merger Mercedes 24/100/140 with its single-overhead-camshaft straight-six engine into the K, which many assumed translated to *kompressor* for the supercharger. The factory,

however, used it to mean *kurz*, or "short," referencing the wheelbase that had been chopped more than a foot from its predecessor, to a still-lengthy 133.9 inches. With fine tuning and blower engaged, 160 bhp was generated and 95.4 mph was achieved, making this new Mercedes-Benz, as the company advertised, the fastest production car in the world.

But brave was the soul who got behind the wheel of the Mercedes-Benz K. Its roadholding was lamentable, and its brakes worse, leading to such sobriquets as "The Flying Death Trap" and "Widow Maker." These defects were remedied in the S (Sport), which moved the K's radiator and engine rearward approximately twelve inches for better weight distribution. The frame was dipped further down between

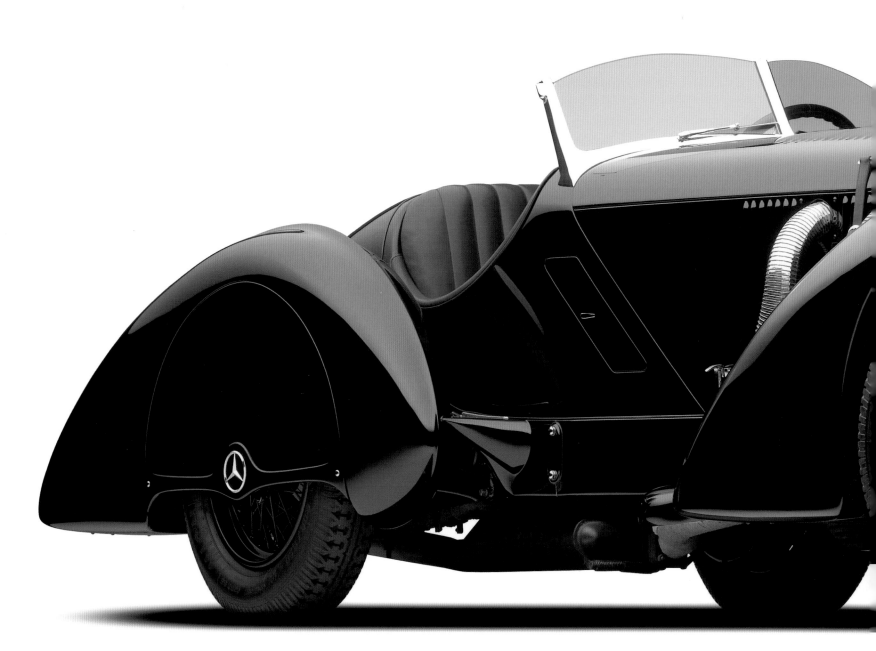

the axles for a lower center of gravity, which additionally improved handling, a good idea since horsepower of the big six had been raised to a supercharged 180. Factory ace Rudi Caracciola won the inaugural at the new circuit near Nurburg castle, followed by victories in the Baden-Baden races and at Britain's Shelsley Walsh, among others. On the last two pages of its Model S catalogue, Daimler-Benz totaled up twenty-seven wins and ten records set by the sports car in its maiden year.

The rich and the famous on both sides of the Atlantic flocked to the Mercedes-Benz S. In New York the car was promoted for its "silent streams of super-power . . . unbounded flexibility [and] comfort to carry you to the ends of the earth." But Hollywood drew more sales.

Al Jolson bought two, one for himself, one for wife Ruby Keeler. Aperitif magnate Andre Dubonnet had one in his garage in Paris. Orders arrived from maharajahs in India.

Next, Dr. Porsche took horsepower to 225 with the SS (for "super" in English-speaking markets), and that was as far as he went. At a board meeting in October 1928, when he was on the losing end of an argument, Porsche lost his cool, loudly, and resigned. He would, of course, be heard from again. His successor, longtime Benz engineer Hans Nibel, made the SSK out of Porsche's S/SS, taking the radiator from the former, the 7.1-liter engine (a tad under 428 cubic inches) from the latter.

The rationale for the SSK was a machine that could win hill climbs easily. The SS measured

an engineer and a good businessman. In the thirties he financially supported Enzo Ferrari's stable of racing Alfa Romeos and served Scuderia Ferrari as president and race driver, the latter quite prominently.

Mercedes were his mounts in the twenties, however, and his training wheels in competition. He is known to have raced in hill climbs with Daimler's cars prior to this glorious automobile. What distinguishes the SSK of Count Trossi is its coachwork. Factory SSKs were delivered with spartan cycle-fendered bodies that perched spare tires on their rear decks. Count Trossi drew the sketch from which this body was crafted and took it to a British coachbuilder to be made into reality. What was curt in the factory body became voluptuous in this one. Hollow-formed and crested pontoon fenders were mated to a body extended to carry the line of function to the rakish V-shaped windshield. Hood and radiator were gracefully lowered. Matching ridges highlighted the sweep of the rear fenders and tapered tail, and made a cohesive whole of the design. Clever touches were the sculpted panel between the frame horns and the styling of the Mercedes three-pointed star into the panel and the jaunty rear wheel spats.

Count Trossi's SSK represents the art of panel beating at its zenith. The coachbuilder's name was White, either Willie or Willy. He is, to date, totally unknown except for this automobile.

— BRK

more than eleven feet between the axles and weighed more than two tons, which was a handful to wield up a hill or on a short circuit. The K this time really did mean short, indicating the truncating of the SS chassis to a comely 116 inches. Teutonic engineering said that to build strong one had to build heavy, and the SSK obliged with 3,700+ pounds, which it immediately began to throw around. Rudi Caracciola adored the car. He won upward of two dozen hill climbs over the next two seasons.

Production of these supercharged Mercedes was minimal; 128 for the S, 111 for the SS, few more than thirty for the SSK. Only a handful, all for factory use, were made of the SSKL, designating *leicht*, or "light" (comparatively), and realized by the copious drilling of holes in the chassis to pare off 250 pounds. Thus ended the series.

Until the effects of the stock market crash rippled across the Atlantic, further devastating Germany's economy, Wilhelm Kissel looked upon these supercharged cars as splendid publicity for his company, which now approached an annual output of 9,000 cars. In addition to the factory competition efforts, the S series cars were raced by their private owners, the "gentleman drivers" who had graced competition from the inception of the automobile. Many, like the original owner of the car shown here, were members of the aristocracy.

Count Carlo Felice Trossi ("Didi" to his intimates) liked speedboats, airplanes, and automobiles. Unlike many of his peers, he was

1955 MERCEDES-BENZ 300SL GULLWING COUPE

DAIMLER-BENZ advertised the 300SL Gullwing as "the best performing production model ever to be offered the public." Rob Walker, the well-known English race sponsor/manager, was more emphatic: "I think it must be the greatest road car that was ever built." Logic tells us that an automobile of this historic magnitude must have been the result of careful planning, but it wasn't. The 300SL was an expedient, pure and simple.

Two weeks of saturation bombing by the U.S. Eighth Air Force in September 1944 had leveled the Daimler-Benz factory. In 1945 the world's oldest automobile company "ceased to exist," in the words of Daimler-Benz executives following their appraisal of the facilities that were now "endless fields of ruin." Less than two weeks after V-E Day, more than 1,200 workers arrived to wield picks, shovels, axes, and bare hands in a massive cleanup. Amazingly, once the rubble was removed, many of the factory machines underneath were found intact.

Repairing trucks for the American Army occupied Daimler-Benz workers until permission was received in the spring of 1946 to return to manufacture. By year's end 214 vehicles left the line, increased to 1,045 in 1948. By 1950 the recovery was well under way, with production at 33,906 units, the highest annual output in the company's history.

Bringing Mercedes back to the exalted position it held in motor sport before the war became a new priority. A grand prix car for 1954 was in development, but another car was needed to keep the Mercedes name alive in the sporting news in the meantime. A competition sports car was the obvious answer.

Enter Rudi Uhlenhaut, the company's development engineer, a Ferdinand Porsche without the tantrums. In the twenties, with the S series, Porsche had crafted a winning racer from a production car; Uhlenhaut would do the same with the new Mercedes 3-liter production sedan, the 300. Wringing the SL (Super Leicht) out of the 300 required wizardry.

The son of a banker, Uhlenhaut had begun his Daimler-Benz career in the experimental department in the early thirties. Fritz Nallinger, a test pilot during World War I, was his boss. They worked well together. Soon Nallinger put him in charge of Mercedes competition cars. In charge of Mercedes design was Karl Wilfert, a company veteran of a quarter century, with his right-hand stylist Friedrich Geiger. How well this quartet succeeded with their assignment was demonstrated by 300SL victories at Le Mans, the Nürburgring, and in the punishing Carrera Panamericana, the 2,000+ mile endurance contest more popularly known as the Mexican Road Race.

Turning a race car that had evolved from a sedan back into a production car required even more wizardry. The pièce-de-résistance of the 300SL was its tubular geodetic, or space, frame, soon to become the norm in competition cars. Welded of myriad small tubes resembling a sophisticated erector set, the construction left no room for traditional entry/egress and led to the most singular feature of the 300SL's styling—its "airplane type" doors, as journalists said on first look. Race rules dictated that

The space frame of the 300SL was constructed from thin tubes of steel welded together in a basic triangular pattern. While the frame combined the virtues of great stability with low weight, the design could not accommodate the height of conventional car doors. This "disadvantage" was the cause for the "gullwings" to be used instead.

doors should open but didn't say how, so the 300SL's did so vertically. With both doors open, a seagull was suggested, and the more evocative "Gullwing" stuck.

Like every other aspect of the design, the Gullwing doors were there because they were the practical solution to a problem. The 300SL had been made as a coupe simply for the higher speeds it would offer over an open roadster down the long Mulsanne straight at Le Mans. Aerodynamics remained the rationale for the production 300SL's body. No protrusions, no door handles, no outside rear-view mirror, no appurtenances impede the flow of air. The car is round all over, as if a straight line would be a sin. The small flares over each wheel help keep the car clean. Engine compartment air vents through the rectangular ports in each side; two ports positioned above the rear window vent interior air. Stepping over the wide body sill and getting oneself seated inside is facilitated by the tilting steering wheel. For females wearing the knee-length straight skirts of the mid-fifties, however, "a delightful display of nylon," in *Autosport* correspondent John Bolster's fine phrase, was unavoidable.

The 300SL design was clean without being boring; it had the look of power but without brutality. Interestingly, the car was less powerful

III. Carrera Panamericana Mexico
Triumphaler Doppelsieg
1. Karl Kling 2. Hermann Lang
Im härtesten 5-Tage-Kampf siegt überlegen in neuer Strecken-Rekordzeit der „Typ 300 SL", entwickelt aus den serienmäßigen Personenwagen von
MERCEDES-BENZ

"Triumphant double victory" at the third Carrera Panamericana race in Mexico, 1952. The race was the toughest of its time, covering 3,371 kilometers on the poorest of roads.

than it appeared. The bhp of the production Gullwing was actually increased (to 215 from 170+) over the race version, thanks to the adoption of fuel injection for the first time in a production car. Performance was not increased, however, because nearly a thousand pounds had been added to the car's weight. The SL was no longer "super leicht." Still, it was good for 135 mph and closed in on 150 with the proper rear-axle ratio, quite sufficient to blow the conventional doors off most other sports cars on the road. Acceleration was astonishing. Paul O'Shea won back-to-back Sports Car Club of

America Class D National Championships in his Gullwing. Among sports car manufacturers, only Ferrari was on the same performance page as this Mercedes.

Some caviled about the car's handling. "A wicked and vicious final-oversteering monster," said one; "a car where a narrow speed band differentiates between going around and turning round," said another. But the Gullwing's race record in both professional and amateur hands demonstrated that many people got the hang of driving one. It was as dangerous as romance, one enthusiast said; a wild

animal one tamed without breaking its spirit was an analogy. The 300SL did not suffer fools gladly but if one wanted to learn how to drive fast, this was the car to teach you. How quickly, if at all, such early owners as movie star Glenn Ford and bandleader Skitch Henderson learned is anyone's guess. Sophia Loren drove a Gull-wing 300SL around her native Naples. Zsa Zsa Gabor was gifted one by Porfirio Rubirosa. Rafael Trujillo, Jr., used his dictator father's money to purchase his.

The Gullwing 300SL was not a moneymaker for Daimler-Benz, but it was not expected to be. The car's purpose was to reintroduce the marque to the sporting world. With its smaller companion 190SL roadster, the 300SL Gull-wing was the first Mercedes to have its world premiere in America, at the International Motor Sports Show in New York in February 1954. Of the 1,400 Gullwing Mercedes manufactured, 900 of them arrived on these shores. To own one for many was to realize a fantasy that even Walter Mitty might not have dared to dream.

— BRK

1958 MERCEDES-BENZ 300SL ROADSTER

L EGEND HAS IT the 300SL Gullwing was made into a production car because of one man: Max Hoffman, the Austrian emigré who had arrived in the New World to sell the cars of the Old World. His timing—June 1941—made that impossible. So Maxie, as he was called, borrowed $300.00 to launch into the manufacture of costume jewelry, which netted him a nest egg sizable enough to get back to what he really wanted to do after V-J Day. Henceforth, all of his jewels would be automobiles.

By the early fifties Hoffman had imported virtually every fine car produced overseas by more than a dozen European manufacturers. A race driver of modest pretension, he was an enthusiast first and last, and very impressed with the racing 300SL. As the story goes, he told Daimler-Benz that if a production version was built, he could sell a thousand of them, ergo the Gullwing car that debuted, and created a sensation, at the Fourth Regiment Armory in New York in February 1954.

But Maxie did not give himself credit for the decision of a Gullwing for the marketplace. He later recalled using the thousand-car figure, but said the idea emanated in Germany. Hoffman insisted to his deathbed, however, that the 190SL roadster introduced alongside the Gullwing was his doing, and so was the open version of the 300SL. Rudi Uhlenhaut corroborated.

In California (particularly Hollywood with its plethora of stars who were Hoffman's regular customers) as well as other sun-drenched sections of the country, coursing in a sports

car through hills or along boulevards without a wind-through-the-hair sensation had begun to pall. And being enwombed in a two-seat body with a lowish ceiling did not appeal to those with a leaning toward the claustrophobic, thus the open car was prepared with the American market in mind—and to please Maxie, an important customer. Fortunately Daimler-Benz had the car all along. Built alongside the W196 Grand Prix Mercedes, the SLS was, typically, the answer to a problem: a car for sprint races that did not require the wind-cheating aerodynamics of the coupe. Three of these roadsters had contested the sports car race accompanying the German Grand Prix at the Nürburgring, and finished one-two-three. "Vastly entertaining," said *The Motor*, the "Mercedes SL/300, in open form, dominated . . . with ease." For the Carrera Panamericana that followed, one of the SLS roadsters was provided to John Fitch, the lanky American driver who had suggested the race to Alfred Neubauer

and who was too tall to comfortably fit in the coupe. The other two team cars were Gullwings.

With the directive for a production open-car version of the 300SL, the Daimler-Benz quartet—Uhlenhaut, Nallinger, Wilfert, Geiger—sprang into action. Amusingly, management feared the 300SL was so identified by the Gull-wing that the design team was asked to make an aluminum hardtop with mini upswept doors for the new open car. (A hardtop would ulti-mately be provided but without the gullwings.)

With the production SLS ready, the next or-der of business was its launch. Marketing man-agers approached David Douglas Duncan. One of the fathers of photojournalism, Duncan had become famous for the World War II photo-graphs he took as a second lieutenant in the Marines. Hired by *Life* in 1946, and in demand by magazines everywhere, he began traveling the world with his camera. Like his good friend Pablo Picasso, Duncan was a Gullwing owner. On one of his visits to the factory, he was asked to do an article on the SLS.

What an inspiration this was. In his photo essay, published in the mass-market weekly *Collier's*, Duncan wrote of Daimler-Benz test drivers "crouched low over the wheel of a silver-blue underslung blur of chrome and steel . . . road-checking their top secret car." His photo-graphs were equally evocative: the SLS career-ing around a hairpin turn at Stelvio Pass, on the cobbled streets of Weil der Stadt, during gravel-road tests in Italy. "The SLS Super Light Special . . . stands but 33 inches high at the door cowling," Duncan wrote, "lower than the ears of the police dogs assigned to guard it."

In its December 1956 issue *Road & Track* ed-itors didn't disguise their chagrin at having been scooped. Two issues later *R&T* published what was called the "first true (not distorted) photo" of the car, and the editors delighted in commenting that it would not be called the SLS but the 300SL Roadster. The car itself arrived at the Geneva Automobile Show shortly there-after, in March 1957.

Whereas the Gullwing was Teutonic and pur-poseful, the Roadster was glamorous and com-fortable. The designation was a misnomer

because the car was a convertible with roll-up windows and offered such creature amenities as actual luggage space, of all things. The frame redesign had lowered the cowhide-covered doorsill by half, reducing the display of nylon among female passengers, and the handling was so nimble one's maiden aunt would not be intimidated. A contemporary road test talked of "a lightness of control that amounts to del-icacy," which probably amused Gullwing driv-ers, some of whom labeled the Roadster a "boudoir on wheels."

At 3,040 pounds (200 more than the coupe), Roadster performance suffered, but 130 miles an hour was still better than offered elsewhere save for the most rarefied quarters. The factory built a competition version of the Roadster for Gullwing champ Paul O'Shea to race against Ferrari, Maserati, and Aston Martin in SCCA's Class D. O'Shea dominated the season, amass-ing three times the championship points of sec-ond place finisher Carroll Shelby in a Maserati.

With both the Gullwing and the Roadster, Daimler-Benz inaugurated its own school of design, borrowing the sleek tautness of Ital-ian lines and mixing it with the no-nonsense rationality that had been a hallmark of the Mer-cedes for a century. A total of 1,858 Mercedes 300SL Roadsters were produced from 1957 to 1962. Daimler-Benz made money on every one of them.

— BRK

The same production line used for the 300SL Gullwing Coupe at Mercedes's Sindelfingen plant was used for the Roadster beginning in 1957.

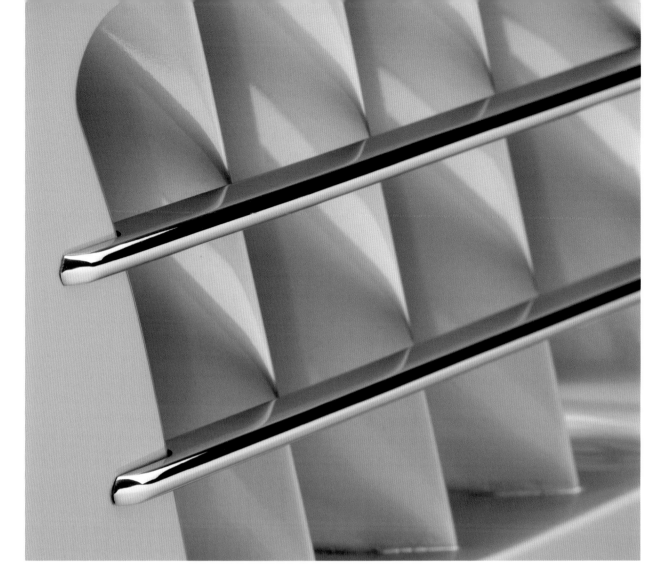

1931 ALFA ROMEO MONZA 8C 2300

T HE FILM *The Graduate* brought the words "Alfa Romeo" into mainstream American consciousness in 1969. The open-air Duetto driven by Dustin Hoffman seduced us with its cute, sleek looks and lovely exhaust note. But Americans were late to the party: Alfa had been bedazzling Europe's elite for decades. And even on our shores, there were some who *did* know. "Every time I see an Alfa Romeo," Henry Ford had famously said in 1939, "I lift my hat."

Alfa Romeo was founded in 1910 on the outskirts of Milan. Its original name was ALFA (Anonima Lombardo Fabbrica Automobili, or Lombard Automobile Factory, Inc.), and it first manufactured airplane engines and large, sturdy cars. Five years later, Nicola Romeo became ALFA's majority shareholder. From a

The winning Alfa Romeo 8c 2300 at Bobbio-Passo del Penice Hill Climb, June 14, 1931.

financial perspective, the thirty-nine-year-old industrialist's timing was perfect. Munitions, war material, and tractor production replaced automobiles when Italy entered World War I, and the workforce ballooned to twenty-five hundred. A surge in operating revenue followed.

After the Armistice, the company changed its name to Alfa Romeo, and automotive production resumed. Almost immediately the firm was beset by the same cash flow and labor problems that had plagued it before the war. The crisis was resolved in part by the intervention of Prime Minister Benito Mussolini, a keen auto enthusiast. Several years later, in fact, the government would become the company's owner.

In 1923 Alfa started wooing fans with the R.L., an all-new model capable of winning important races such as the Targa Florio, and by the following year the company became a magnet for star personnel in the auto industry. Its payroll boasted engineers Luigi Bazzi and Vittorio Jano and drivers Enzo Ferrari, Giuseppe Campari, and Antonio Ascari. This cadre of men and the Targa Florio victory convinced Nicola Romeo that continued participation in international races was the best way to promote the marque.

But there was more to Alfas than just speed. In the mid-1920s, these cars were on the leading edge of an evolution from simple means of transportation to art objects. Their road manners were just as alluring.

One of the first was the 6C 1500, with a body made by the company of Ugo Zagato, a coachbuilder who specialized in lightweight, aerodynamically efficient bodies on cars. In many ways the relationship between Alfa and Zagato was like that of a patron commissioning a sculptor to work his magic with metal. Alfa test driver Giovanbattista Guidotti honored both the car's handling and its looks when he told Italian journalist Michele Marchiano, "It seemed like it was glued to the road even when we encountered stretches of gravel. Driving it gave me a new feel: that of total security. To look at her was like looking at a work of art."

By the late 1920s, Zagato-bodied Alfas were dominating sporting events such as the Mille Miglia, a grueling thousand-mile race through Italy on public roads. The race's appeal quickly became so great that hundreds of thousands of Italians would come out to watch, their fanaticism making America's love of football pale in comparison. Everyone had his or her favorite driver and, just as important, preferred manufacturer. Alfa's string of victories and the resulting publicity were a crucial part of its reputation for producing outstanding "dual-purpose" cars, machines that appealed to both top drivers in serious competition and amateur sportsmen (such as Zagato-Alfa owner Mussolini) who simply wanted to go fast on the road. By the early 1930s, however, the 6C was facing serious competition from rival brands such as Mercedes, so Alfa engineer Jano created a masterpiece of an 8-cylinder engine that featured a supercharger for extra power. The resulting 8C 2300 model (referring to its 8-cylinder engine with 2300-cc capacity) started the legend of 8C Alfa Romeos.

In the 1920s and particularly the 1930s, cars were often constructed like a fine suit, tailored to the client's specifications and whims. The manufacturer would make the chassis and then install the suspension, drive train (engine and transmission), and wheels so that the car could move under its own power. A client could order the 8C with a long or short chassis, depending upon the car's purpose. The long chassis offered more space and was typically used on more luxurious cars, while the short chassis was the mainstay of those interested mainly in speed. Once the client purchased the chassis,

Poster for the twelfth annual Mille Miglia, April 1938, detailing the streets on which the race would be held, and advising pedestrians and cyclists to observe "maximum caution."

he normally took it to an independent coach-builder such as Zagato. Some 8Cs had stunning bodies with swooping fender lines, beautiful curves, and intricate details that any fan of art deco would appreciate. Others were designed to be light and efficient, keeping ornamentation to a minimum.

The 8C shown here is one of the latter. The torpedo body looks like an airplane fuselage—narrow in the front, widening slightly as it moves to the rear, typical of grand prix cars in the early 1930s. The headlights, bracing, and mudguards over the wheels were added when the Alfa began endurance racing. Historian Simon Moore has shown that the car, chassis 2111043, raced from the start and participated in six grand prix in 1932, winning one.

One touch added much later is the visually enticing "SF" shield on the hood. Art often has meaningful symbolism, and the same can be said for cars. This crest carries special significance in Alfa and auto history, as it was only worn by cars raced by Enzo Ferrari's Scuderia Ferrari.

Ferrari's name is perhaps the most famous in automotive history, linked with the legendary company and cars he created after World War II. What is often overlooked is that he made his reputation—the one that put him

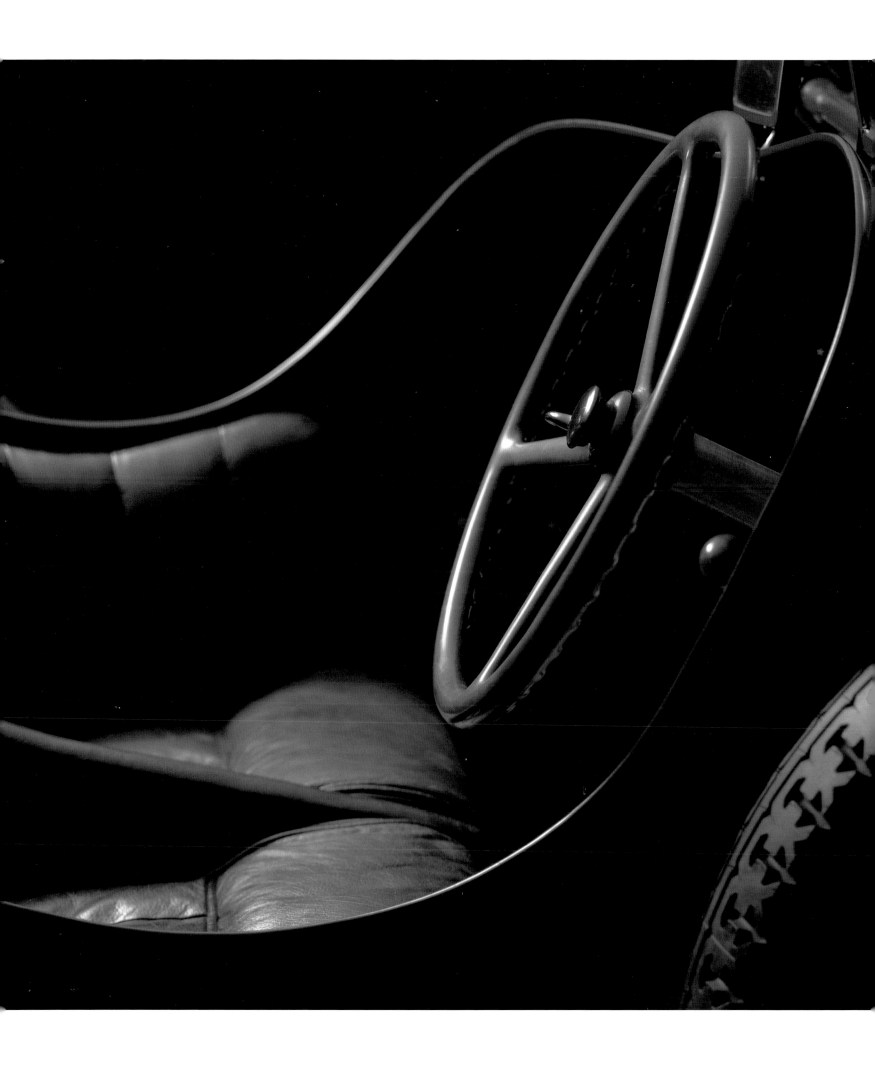

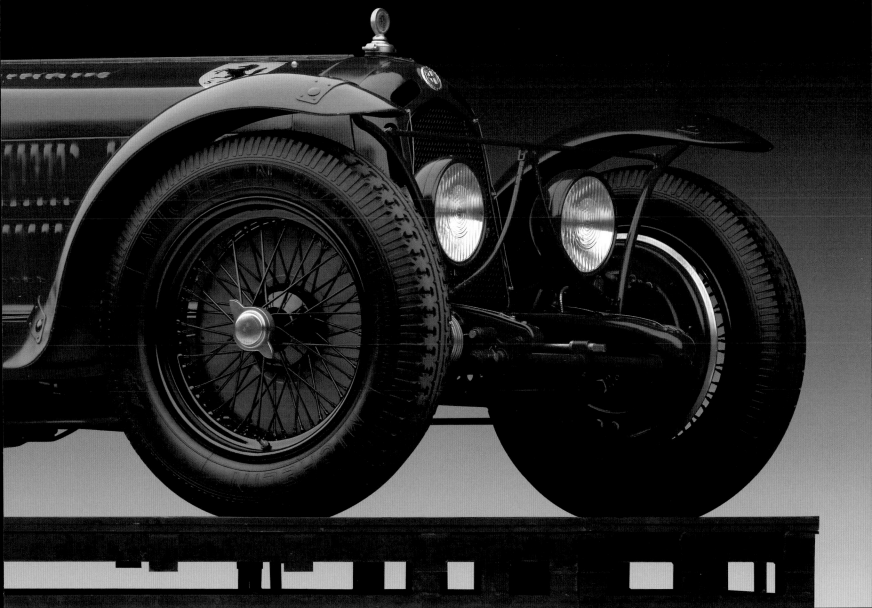

in the position to create his own machines—at Alfa Romeo. He had joined Alfa as a racing driver in 1920, enjoying intermittent competition success during that decade but proving even better behind the scenes. In addition to luring noted engineers Luigi Bazzi and Vittorio Jano from Fiat, a much larger company, Ferrari helped instigate one of Alfa's earliest performance models, the 20/30 ES Sport.

As the decade came to a close, Ferrari understood that his future was not in the seat of a racing car. "I found myself overwhelmed by an almost morbid desire to do something for the motor car, for this creature I was passionately fond of," he wrote. "So although I was doing well enough to justify pursuing a driving career, I had my sights set on wider, more ambitious horizons." Then one night at a dinner party, Ferrari and two well-to-do auto enthusiasts decided to form a company that would prepare their own cars and offer technical support. The Scuderia Ferrari ("Ferrari racing stable") was born in the autumn of 1929.

From the outset, the Scuderia Ferrari competed using Alfa's fastest cars. Not only did Ferrari have the Alfa franchise for the region where he resided, but Alfa Romeo never saw him as a competitor. Rather, the Scuderia was more like an association of ultra-loyal Alfa clients who shared a passion for racing as well as engineering and financial interests. Ferrari kept Alfa informed about his and the competition's developments.

The arrangement's benefits were soon obvious. According to historian Luigi Orsini, the Scuderia entered twenty-two races in 1930, scoring eight victories. Enzo Ferrari was now a celebrity, something he never achieved as a racing driver. The colorful prancing horse and Scuderia Ferrari badge certainly helped, keeping his name present in the minds of competitors and enthusiasts everywhere.

When Alfa announced its withdrawal from single-seat racing in 1933, Enzo persuaded the company to let him continue developing and racing its cars. "You have to understand the period to [grasp] the enormity of what Ferrari accomplished," racing ace René Dreyfus told Orsini. "There had never been anything like the team he had, never anything that big and so well organized . . . [Despite] interference from the Fascists [and] personality problems and rivalries within the team . . . there was no doubt he was the 'Boss'—and the only Boss . . . The Scuderia was his dream . . . He was the whole thing."

But it couldn't last forever. The Alfa-Ferrari marriage began unraveling in 1937, after clashes with personnel inside Alfa. In his memoirs Ferrari notes that Alfa's managing director Ugo Gobbato preferred planning everything down to the last detail, while Ferrari believed in working with a small group that responded quickly under a flexible management structure. By 1939 the situation had become untenable and the Scuderia was liquidated. Ferrari also signed a clause that stated he could not produce a car under his own name for four years.

After World War II, Ferrari would go on to achieve even greater fame as a constructor of his own cars. The Alfa legend continued as well, the company remaining at the top of its game in the late 1940s and early 1950s. Alfas would win the grand prix circuit's first two world championships in 1950 and 1951—a fitting testament to the greatness of prewar machines such as the 8C 2300.

—WSG

1938 ALFA ROMEO 8C 2900 MILLE MIGLIA

WHEN IT COMES TO prewar automobiles, Alfa's 8C 2900 shows the creative process at its finest. The model was a natural evolution of the 8C 2300 in Alfa's never-ending quest for speed, and the mechanical components underneath its skin are so beautiful, and so lovingly handcrafted, that any jeweler would smile in appreciation.

But it is the body covering the engine and chassis that everyone sees, and here the case of form following function is nothing short of breathtaking. The eye instinctively moves from front to rear, so perfect is the symmetry and sweep of the body panels. The wheels, covered by teardrop-shaped fenders, are themselves works of art. The tapering tail is like the back of a beautiful woman.

The man behind the work is Felice Bianchi Anderloni. The third child of prominent railway engineer Emilio Anderloni and his wife, Linda, he was born in Rome on April 28, 1884. Felice wanted to become an engineer like his father but his strong-willed mother pushed him to study law, her rationale being he could obtain a law degree more quickly. Following her wishes, he graduated in 1904, but rarely used his degree. He had been interested in cars since his teens and that passion would see him become one of the prewar era's greatest, most influential "stylists," as designers were then known.

Anderloni's first automotive employer was Isotta Fraschini, one of Italy's great luxury car manufacturers. Anderloni soon proved his mettle and was appointed chief of the company's

Opposite:
Ralph Lauren's Alpha 8C 2900 mid-restoration by Paul Russell, Essex, Massachusetts, May 2004.

Hugh Hunter crossing the finish line in his Alfa Romeo 8c 2900 (winner of the previous year's Mille Miglia) at the Lewes Speed Trials, August 1939.

Alfa 8c 2900 no. 148 at the Mille Miglia Brescia, 1938.

experimental and testing department; later he sold and marketed Isotta's products. He was also a capable gentleman racer who competed elegantly adorned in a bow tie and beautifully tailored suits. His fame would come not as an engineer, driver, or marketing whiz, however, but as the head of one of Italy's great coach-building firms. In 1925 he and his friend Gaetano Ponzoni purchased Carrozzeria Falco, an ailing coachbuilding company, and the following year he changed the name to Carrozzeria Touring, as "Touring" was a word easily recognized throughout the world.

From this point on, Anderloni's life revolved more passionately than ever around the automobile. His son Carlo remembers realizing that his father was doing something extraordinary because pedestrians frequently stopped to ogle the Touring-bodied machine parked on the street in front of their apartment building.

Felice's creations also drew attention in northern Italy's *concorso d'eleganza* circuit. These automotive "beauty contests" had existed during the previous decade, but in the 1930s Mussolini's government actively promoted them. Meanwhile, as author Luciano Greggio points out, Italian consumers were catching on to the benefits of style, and began demanding cars that would establish the difference between themselves and others who were

fortunate enough to possess a private means of transport: "Demand for the custom-built special, with all that the term implies in terms of perceived social status and social climbing, was beginning to make itself felt." The *concorso* flourished, and garnered considerable attention because coachbuilders such as Touring displayed their most recent works in competition with one another. Since car companies during this period frequently sold only the chassis, the customer's choice of coachbuilder, and the relative differences in style and expertise among the various coachbuilding firms became all the more important.

The *concorso* was held three to four times a year at elegant resorts such as Lake Como's luxurious Villa d'Este. Both the jury, composed of motorcar industry VIPs, and the public judged the car's interior and exterior from an aesthetic point of view and would award a prize to the most beautiful car. Helping to propel the contest to national prominence was the fashion industry. Clothing designers would debut apparel and provide models—all done to complement the car being shown.

A fashion show and an exhibition of art and industrial style all rolled into one, the *concorso d'eleganza* truly came of age in 1931, the year that Carrozzeria Touring debuted its ground-breaking "Flying Star." Felice smartly applied art deco chrome trim touches to spectacular effect on the car's all-white body (white being a fashionable color in clothing that year). The proportioning of its shape and new running

This Alfa 8C 2900 during a pit stop in the Mille Miglia, 1938. The booted soldier hovering near the car is a reminder that Mussolini's government owned the Alfa Romeo company in those years.

board treatment had other designers rushing to copy it. But cars such as 8C 2900 chassis number 412030 (the model shown here) demonstrate how aerodynamic efficiency directed Felice's eye. Touring's ability to create beautiful yet disparate designs came from its patented *superleggera*, or "super light," construction technique. The system used a frame of small-diameter steel tubes to support the car's aluminum body. This inherent suppleness allowed Anderloni to design and construct shapes that were more rounded than those of other coachbuilders.

The *superleggera* technique originated in France. In 1922 the aviator Charles Weymann pioneered a new system for building lightweight car bodies, and Anderloni acquired the rights to use it toward the end of the decade. Over time, Touring developed its own version, and by the end of the 1930s had patented the tech-

nique, allowing Felice the freedom to create a series of sensational shapes on the 8C 2900 that dominated the *concorso* and racing scenes.

The process was an arduous one. Carlo said his father would often wake at night, turn on the light and start sketching away on the pad beside the bed. Once his ideas were completed, Anderloni turned to his "visualizers," artisans inside Touring who would make his concepts reality with larger scale, even full-scale, drawings. Other craftsmen then created the car body by hand and placed it on the chassis. To test the aerodynamics, the completed car was covered in felt strips and taken on the road, with a cameraman in a second car snapping pictures to record how the wind flowed over the form. Rare in the prewar period, this technique would become *de rigueur* in the 1950s and 1960s, until wind-tunnel testing became prevalent.

These techniques were undoubtedly used on this 8C 2900, which, along with three other identical 8Cs, was built for the 1938 Mille Miglia. Alfa dominated the race, and chassis number 412030 led for most of the thousand-mile contest. Near the end, a brake problem sidelined it for fourteen minutes, causing it to finish second by a mere two seconds.

These immortal Alfas proved to be the zenith in prewar sports and racing car construction. Within two years Italy was embroiled in World War II, causing design, development, and construction of such machines to cease. Fittingly, when the first postwar Mille Miglia was run in 1947, another Touring-bodied 8C 2900 took the checkered flag.

—wsg

1933 BUGATTI TYPE 59 GRAND PRIX

THE TYPE 59 BUGATTI, the linear successor to the Types 51 and 54, was built from 1933 to 1936. Marginally more successful than its predecessors, it was less successful than the antecedent Type 35 and its variations of the previous decade. What makes the Type 59 worthy of note is its place in history as the last series grand prix car produced in the Bugatti factory—and that it is, to many, the prettiest race car ever built. Others opt for the Type 35. Few choose a racer that was not built in the small Alsatian village of Molsheim that was Ettore Bugatti's fiefdom.

Bugatti was an architect, horseman, shipbuilder, aero-engineer, locomotive builder, farmer, vintner, fashion designer, and manufacturer of automobiles. Mostly he was an artist. Growing up in Milan, he is said to have believed himself lesser in talent to his father Carlo, a painter, silversmith, and noted furniture designer, and his brother Roland, a sculptor. Psychologists might tell us these feelings of inferiority were the reason he strove so mightily to excel in motor sport.

Ettore Bugatti was drawn to racing initially because it paid better. His talents had been noticed in 1901 by Baron Eugen de Dietrich, proprietor of a small automobile factory in Neidebronn, Alsace, Germany. Like many members of the nobility, de Dietrich was enthralled with the new invention called the automobile, most especially pitting his own against his peers' in competition. To encourage his new young engineer, he offered Bugatti a royalty four times greater for a race car than for one the baron or his customers might drive

Ettore Bugatti in 1900.

on the road. Bugatti obliged, producing designs that looked like proper race cars but were not very reliable, which ultimately distressed the baron, so he fired his designer and quit the automobile business.

Remaining in Alsace, Ettore freelanced from an office on the top floor of the Hôtel de Paris in Graffenstaden until mid-1907, when he accepted the position of chief engineer of Deutz Gasmotoren Fabrik in Cologne. To overcome the boredom of working in a large factory, Bugatti built a car in the basement of his home. Deutz conveniently found it necessary to break

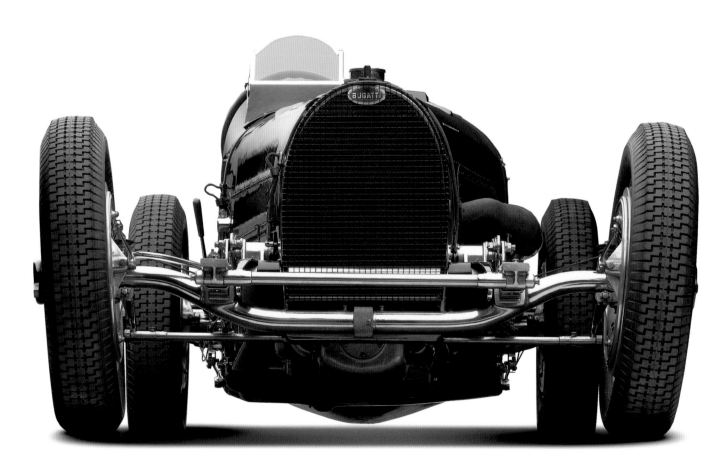

his contract, giving him a substantial severance, so Bugatti piled his wife and children into the basement prototype and drove from Cologne to Alsace in search of a factory. With the help of colleague Ernest Friderich and a friendly banker named Vizcaya, he would now become an automaker. An abandoned dye works was acquired in Molsheim. Over Christmas holiday of 1909 Friderich whitewashed the walls inside and out, and Bugatti jumped into his car and drove to Cologne and Paris to buy equipment. Five cars were produced in 1910.

In 1911 Bugatti and Friderich were ready to race in the French Grand Prix at Le Mans. Favorites to win were the Italian and French factory teams of huge cars driven by chain with 4-cylinder engines so tall their drivers often had to peer around rather than over them. The shaft-drive Bugatti's four cylinders were petite by comparison, and the tiny car weighed all of 660 pounds. In seven hours of racing on a blisteringly hot day, as tires melted, engines overheated, and chassis parts broke, the little white Bugatti cooly lapped the circuit and

finished second to one of the few behemoths still running at the end of the race.

Immediate fame brought the immediate problem of expanding the factory fast enough to keep pace with the demand for the car that had kept pace with the giants. Bugatti was coping nicely until World War I intervened. Alsace had been disputed territory since the Franco-Prussian War. That Ettore was an Italian who admired the French and was living in Germany made it a very good idea for him to leave for the duration. The parts of three unassembled race cars were buried there; Bugatti left with his family and two race cars recently completed, which he entombed in the basement of the family home in Milan.

With peace and royalties from an aero-engine design, Bugatti returned to Alsace, which now belonged to France, to rebuild and to race with the five cars that were already six years old. There was only one event in the French racing calendar in 1920: a Voiturette Grand Prix of six hours at Le Mans. Of the three cars that had to be assembled from their parts, two would serve as backup, one would compete

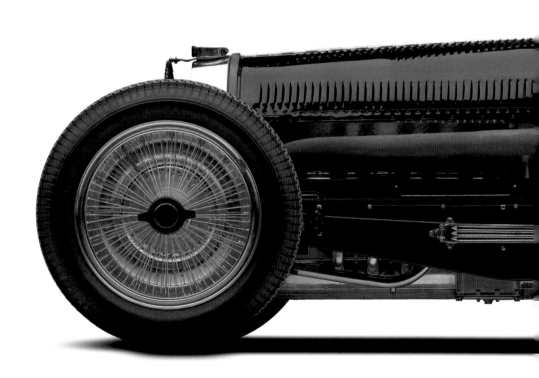

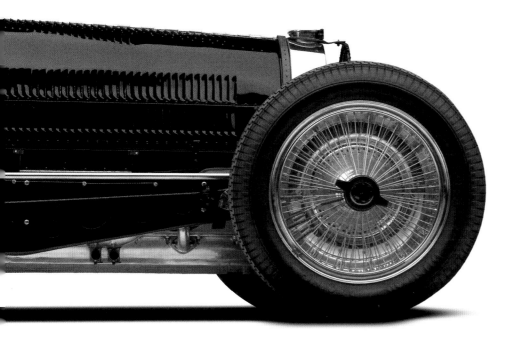
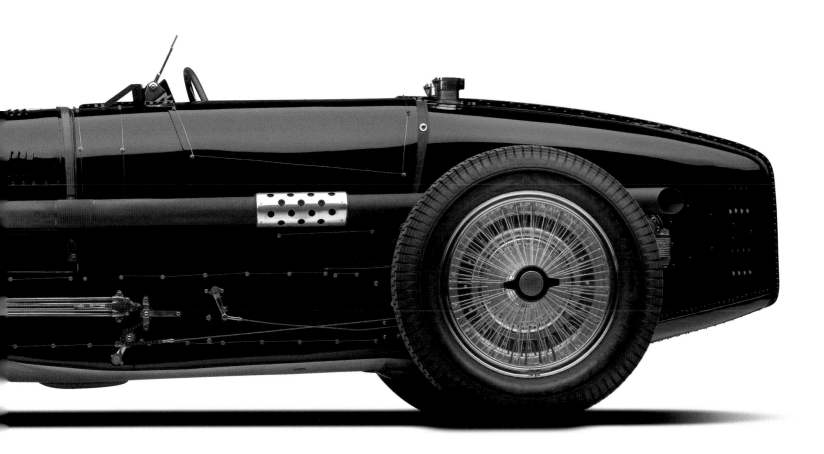

shoe. It was easy to be seduced by the visual loveliness of a Bugatti race car, and Bugatti's sense of the aesthetic was everywhere. But the artist in him was matched by an ego as big as all outdoors. And to win was paramount.

In 1924 and 1925 the Type 35 won 351 races and established forty-seven records. "It is now winning more races than ever, of all kinds and all over Europe," its maker bragged, "simply and easily in the hands of my customers who thus become masterly drivers." In 1926 Bugattis averaged more than fourteen victories a week. By 1928, when the race calendar didn't have enough races to suit him, Bugatti organized one of his own. The Targa Florio was won five years in a row. Grand prix checkered flags, which fell to the Type 35 with alacrity, included the 1929 inaugural of a grand prix through the streets of Monaco. René Dreyfus won the following year with his independently entered Bugatti and was hired for the factory team afterward.

The Bugatti Type 59 driven by Tazio Nuvolari in Monaco, April 1934.

alongside the two Milan cars. A one-two-three finish looked like a possibility, but Ettore, as team manager, squelched that by checking the radiator cap of one car during a pit stop, which the rules said only a mechanic could do, thereby leading to disqualification. Victory went to Ernest Friderich's car.

For the next decade Bugatti race cars would be feared by those who had to compete against them and revered by those who drove them. Unlike other manufacturers who sold replicas of their racers only after they were superseded, Bugatti chose to sell duplicates of his team cars to anyone who asked. The car shown here, for example, was bought in 1935 by Welsh industrialist Lindsay Eccles. This policy swelled the ranks of Bugatti racers and resulted in a record of race victories that to call astonishing is an understatement.

That record began with the 4-cylinder Type 13, which became known as the Brescia for the first race it won. Its class was 1500 cc (free-for-all competitions were no more). To compete in the Grand Prix, the top rung of racing's ladder, Bugatti needed more performance from his car. "Nothing is too good, nothing is too dear," Ettore Bugatti wrote. "You've got to win, whatever the cost; you work day and night if necessary." This all-out effort produced the Type 35, a 2-liter single-overhead-cam 90-hp straight eight that was installed into a chassis of virile beauty fronted by a radiator that Bugatti designed after the archway into Molsheim's city center but that everyone else called a horse-

Bugatti advertising poster designed by Roger Soubie, about 1929.

deeper into a Type 54 chassis lightened by coring holes into its side members. This lowered both the center of gravity and the transmission line, which dictated the attitude of the car overall. As its forebears, the balance of line and proportion of the Type 59 was flawless from the signature grille to the barreled curvature of the body to the long tapering tail.

Most striking were the 59's famous piano-wire wheels, which better defined Ettore Bugatti as an artist-engineer than perhaps any other single component he designed. From the wheel's hub, slender high tensile spokes without the traditional overlapping radiated to a light alloy rim to support the weight of the car and absorb lateral stress when cornering. The flanged aluminum brake drum took both driving and braking torque. The wheels were of exceptionally light construction. And they were gorgeous.

"Ettore Bugatti was crazy about those wheels," René Dreyfus said. "We drivers were not. There were so many splines that when the clutch was let out, the tiny slack between the inside of the wheel rim and the brake drum created a knocking noise that sounded like a loose rear end." This was not a sound the team drivers wanted to hear, and they complained. Their boss just laughed and told them to get used to it. Eventually they did.

The Type 59 was a swan song of the classic European race car. Six, perhaps seven, were built, the low production attributable to the growing reality that further racing was futile if victory was the raison d'être. For all the technical prowess and power of the thundering German machines that overwhelmed the grand prix scene for the remainder of the thirties, they didn't have wheels that even approached the aesthetic appeal of the Type 59's.

—BRK

In 1931 the Type 51, with a 160-hp-twin-cam development of the 35's straight eight, was expected to carry on the glorious winning tradition but it did not. The Monaco Grand Prix was won yet again but the competition had caught up. Bugattis began losing races. The engines were enlarged to 3.3 liters and, when that wasn't enough, to 4.9 in the Type 54.

Mussolini's Italy and Hitler's Germany were by now subsidizing their nations' racing efforts. Der Führer particularly let it be known that the first world he planned to conquer was that of motor sport. Without subsidies, Bugatti was powerless to compete effectively. He brought forth a magnificent machine nonetheless, essentially from his parts bin.

The Type 59's engine was a finely tuned variation of the 3.3 litre Type 57 that was slung

1937 BUGATTI TYPE 57SC GANGLOFF DROP HEAD COUPE

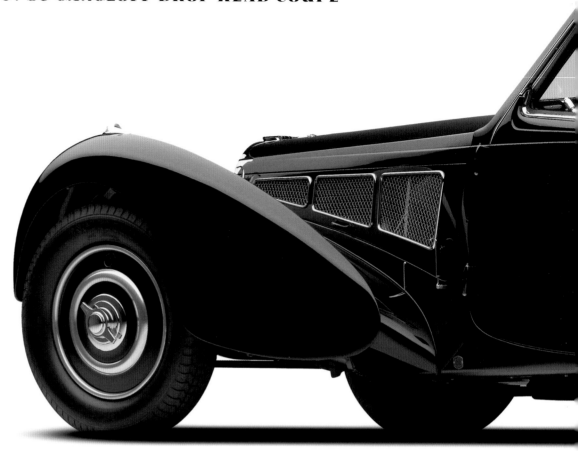

ETTORE BUGATTI once said "A technical creation can only be perfect if it is perfect from the point of view of aesthetics." Following his decision at age sixteen to give up on becoming the artist his father wished him to be, Bugatti brought his art to the automobile.

During the 1890s, throughout Europe and America, the possibilities and promise of individualized motor transport excited the imagination of legions who were compatible with the mechanical. Many began, as did Ettore Bugatti, by buying someone else's machine and making it better. First he took apart the gasoline-powered Prinetti tricycle and put it back together to see how it worked. As soon as he learned how to drive, he took the Prinetti racing and did well, modifying the vehicle after each event to increase its performance. The following year, 1899, he built his own tricycle, with a motor for each rear wheel. He tried the same concept on an automobile he built at the

turn of the century but discovered an engine at each of four wheels was not the way to go. His only training had been art; he had to teach himself engineering.

A good student and a quick study, Bugatti was immediately successful. His third car won a gold medal in the International Sport Exhibition in Milan in 1901, which attracted the attention of Baron de Dietrich who launched him into the automobile business the following year. Eight years later he had his own factory. Extensive outlays for advertising wouldn't be necessary; Bugatti race results spoke volumes to a clientele largely composed of sportsmen who liked to compete. A Bugatti was perfect for them.

For more than two decades, Bugatti focused on fast and light cars with impeccable road holding. A notable exception to this rule was the Type 41, La Royale, with a gargantuan 13-liter engine and a 170-inch wheelbase, that Bugatti planned as a car of state for kings but

that circumstance (the Great Depression largely) caused him to settle for selling only to very rich commoners.

This didn't mean that Ettore Bugatti was willing to sell to just anyone with the money. Indeed he had refused to sell one of his Royales to King Carol II of Romania because he didn't like the man's table manners. And, "Do not let it happen again," he said to a Parisian who brought his Type 46 back to the factory for adjustment a fourth time. A complaint about brakes from another customer brought the rejoinder, "I build my cars to go, not to stop." To the fellow who lamented that his Type 55 was difficult to start in cold weather, he replied, "If you can afford a Bugatti, surely you can afford a heated garage."

Early on, Ettore Bugatti gave himself the sobriquet Le Patron (the Boss). He wore his imperiousness like a badge. Chancing an insult, customers flocked to Molsheim to bask awhile in his kingdom. To divert them, he offered his own museums to visit, one with small arms ranging from cross-bows to Colts that Bugatti had collected, another with animal sculptures by his brother Roland, another of exquisite horse-drawn carriages. And there was always an interesting assemblage of various limousines that had been traded in by the newly initiated.

Bugatti's home was filled with art and household objects he designed, which workmen in the factory would build for him on a moment's notice, shunting aside the work that paid the bills. There were also glorious and inviting Bugatti-designed bronze hinges on the factory doors, but rare was the customer who was allowed through them. Bugatti did not relish customers seeing the more mundane aspects of the creation of his motorcars. His penchant for cleanliness, which resulted in a factory floor that could have been an operating theater, might have been another reason.

A small hotel nearby, where his race drivers

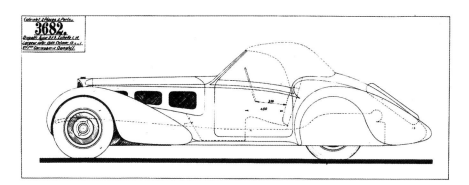

Line drawing from the Bugatti studio of this Type 57SC Gangloff Drop Head Coupe.

French advertisement emphasizing the Bugatti line's "thoroughbred automobiles," in *La Vie Automobile*, July 1924.

stayed, was available to his customers. Ettore Bugatti called it the Hostellerie du Pur Sang (pure blooded, thoroughbred). He dressed the part. Bowler hat and jodhpurs, handsome boots and riding crop, artfully tailored sports jacket (which likely as not he designed himself), Ettore Bugatti astride a blooded horse was the personification of the noble steeds he produced. One mid-twenties advertisement, subtitled *Le pur sang des Automobiles*, didn't depict an automobile at all but pictured one of Le Patron's horses instead. Long before public relations was coined as a phrase, Bugatti had mastered the technique of inventing himself in the glamorous image of his product.

If you were a good customer, he might take you on a shoot. Bugatti raised birds and dogs and horses. He designed saddles to be made in the upholstery shop for both the canines and equines. Bugatti could show you his landscaped gardens, his vineyards, the distillery making Mirabelle liqueur. Or his electrical generating plant. Bugatti's place of business was like no other in the world.

But the man's lifestyle and his obsessions

combined to render him broke most of the time. Sometimes he would whip off a design for another manufacturer to make ends meet. René Dreyfus said factory team drivers were occasionally paid their wages and bonus money with a chassis they drove to the Paris showroom to sell. When his fixation on producing the Type 41 moved the company to the brink of bankruptcy and left a gaggle of 13-liter Royale engines gathering dust in a loft, Jean Bugatti persuaded the government to allow the company to adapt them to power the railway cars that would put France in the forefront of the locomotive field. Barely turned twenty-one, Ettore Bugatti's son, who had been schooled

at home and apprenticed in the factory, guided the company out of hostile waters—and into a new preeminence.

His father had largely created according to whim. "My ideas give me no rest," he once said. Although total production since inception was not yet six thousand cars, they had been manufactured in nearly forty types, sometimes several in production at the same time. Jean brought commercial rationality to the Bugatti factory.

The Type 57 was introduced at the Paris Salon of 1933 and remained the focus of production until World War II, with varying modifications developed for different customer tastes and needs. Jean fashioned a Bugatti for members of the smart set who might not be interested in sporting events. Catalogues hailed "Puissance [strength], Sécurité, Confort, Précision" and purposely left "Vitesse [speed]" out, to give notice that these new Bugattis were as refined as they were fast.

In basic touring-car trim, the 3.3-liter straight-eight engine propelled the Type 57 to 95 mph, quite sufficient for most drivers. For Bugatti's traditional clientele, the 57T (tuned) touched 115 mph, as did the 57C (compressor) for those who needed the surge of supercharging. The 57S, which most owners thought designated Sport (for its shortened and more maneuverable chassis), actually referred to Surbaissé (lowered, which the chassis also was) —and resulted in a Bugatti that topped 120 mph, making it the fastest French production car of the period. Adding supercharging for the 57SC brought 220 hp, 130 mph, and a 0–80 mph acceleration of 19.0 seconds that no other production car anywhere could match. No more than two Type 57SC Bugattis were delivered new from Molsheim. When word passed of the car's capability, a number of owners returned their 57S Bugattis to the factory to be retrofitted with the supercharger, which availed them of a few days at the Pur Sang to hobnob with team drivers and enjoy the factory environs. Philippe Levy, whose family had long been successful in the textile business in Strasbourg, returned the exhibit car to Molsheim for that purpose.

Had Jean Bugatti been a little older he might have been able to convince his father of the wisdom of independent front suspension and

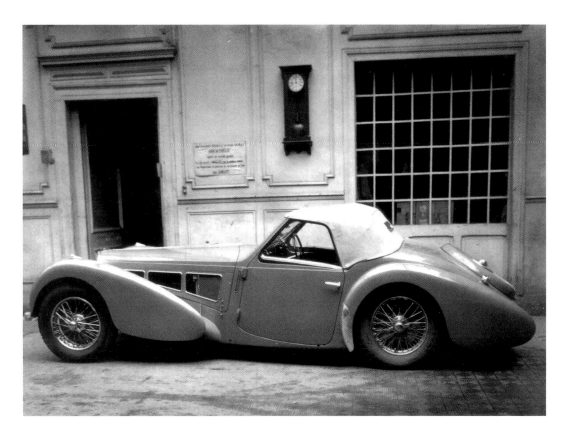

This Bugatti Drop Head Coupe (#57563) at the Gangloff workshop in Colmar, awaiting delivery.

hydraulic brakes. Ettore Bugatti abhorred supercharging for the same reason W. O. Bentley did; that is, it was a spurious way to enhance power, but like W. O. he had gradually warmed to the idea enough to allow it on his cars. But independent front suspension and hydraulics were a tougher sell. So Jean turned his talents to coachwork. The craftsmen at Gangloff, the factory's favored coachbuilder in Colmar about thirty-five miles away, looked askance at the young man, suspecting nepotism was the only reason he was there, until he showed them what he could do.

With the 57 he treaded lightly at first, affixing a new radiator that was a miniature of his father's beloved Royale. The thermostatically controlled shutters in front of the new honeycomb radiator were originally painted to match body color but subsequently were chrome plated to complement the chassis. Coachbuilders then and Bugattistes now argue the merits of the long and relatively high Type 57 chassis for the creation of the soigné aerodynamic bodies coming into vogue. That argument was settled with the 57S that Jean created in 1936 following a strike at the factory, which sent Ettore Bugatti off to set up an atelier in Paris, leaving his son to manage the factory.

With the 57S it was easy enough to shorten the chassis but lowering it required the rear axle to pass through the rear frame, also necessitating a dry sump for engine lubrication to increase road clearance. The flat 57 radiator would look out of place on this new model so Jean designed a lower one in an egg shape that he slightly veed, which, with the headlights incorporated into the wider, taller fenders, intensified the hunkered-down look. From every angle, the Type 57S was a new car. Its profile, like John Barrymore's, was perfect. Jean was just getting started.

— BRK

1938 BUGATTI TYPE 57SC ATLANTIC COUPE

ABOUT 680 Type 57 Bugattis were produced in all of its variations. Of them, few more than forty were the 57S/SC. Atlantics numbered three. It's not difficult to suspect why. The Atlantic was and is the most controversial of all Jean Bugatti's creations. Beauty being in the beholder's eye is relevant. Some see the most beautiful car ever built. Others look upon the Atlantic as outrageous. Few deny that it is brilliant.

The exhibit car was the last Atlantic built, ordered in 1937 by Richard B. Pope, an English barrister, amateur tennis champion, and Bugattiste of the highest order. Great Britain was the Bugatti company's best export market, and Pope was arguably its best British customer. Whenever a new type came out, he had to have one. The Atlantic was his tenth Bugatti. Six of them had been delivered to the Paris showroom on the Champs Elysees. This one the new owner picked up at the factory. A tall man, Pope had asked for an inch more headroom, which could only be provided by raising the roof, which in turn necessitated redrawing the lines of the car and preparing a wooden buck for the coachwork to be made. Jean Bugatti was happy to oblige. The following year Pope returned the car to the factory to be converted from 57S to SC. In nearly thirty years of ownership, he drove his Atlantic 37,500 miles, with no fear of passing another like it on the road.

The inspiration for the Atlantic was the Aérolithe, a show car both lithe and aerodynamic that Jean designed for the Paris Automobile Salon in October 1935. The national press, priding itself on being in the forefront of fashion and accustomed to the cubist and often unpretty automotive confections of the eccentric French automaker Gabriel Voisin, greeted the Aérolithe with wild acclaim. Here was a car that both encapsulated l'art moderne and was a paean to the new school of scientific streamlining. Jean Bugatti was encouraged to press on in his exercise in the futuristic.

Because the Aérolithe used the standard Type 57 chassis and suspension, aerodynamics was compromised by its height and the flat face of the radiator. The Atlantic used the Type 57S chassis, lowered by six inches, and with the V-shaped radiator. The headlights, which were designed into the fender of the Aérolithe, were raised and detached on the Atlantic. The rivets stayed.

Rivets had first appeared on the front fenders and tail of the Type 59 Grand Prix car to solve a manufacturing problem, and they appeared on the Aérolithe for probably the same reason. Whether the body of the show car was made of Elektron (a magnesium alloy) or Duralumin (an aluminum alloy) is open to conjecture, and because the Aérolithe does not survive we shall never be certain. Either alloy was difficult to weld, which, likely as not, led to the exposed seams with button head rivets running down the spine of the body and around the fenders.

Since the Atlantic was made of aluminum, the necessity for riveted flanges vanished but Jean Bugatti kept them anyway because he liked them. He was, after all, his artistic father's son. Their dramatic styling statement paid com-

pliment to the perfect proportion and stance of the car, and drew the eye to other elements of original thinking in the design. Aviation influences were found in the semi-ellipsoidal windows and the doors that were cut well into the roof to make entering the vehicle easier.

Revered Bugatti historian Hugh Conway found the Atlantic "extraordinary, bizarre and interesting, but not perhaps beautiful in any normal sense." Quite so. The two beholders earlier alluded to are perhaps both right. The beauty of the Atlantic is that it is outrageous. The car is, in its essence, a fluid natural form

to which Jean Bugatti deftly added his own flamboyant aesthetic touches.

If Jean considered the driver inside, he could not have thought about him long. Visibility to the sides and rear is virtually nil, "like turning your head inside the hood of a parka," in the delicious simile of motoring journalist David E. Davis, Jr., who drove this Atlantic. The weight of the coupe body over the rear wheels and the positive cambered front wheels make the handling somewhat unpredictable. And conversation is nearly impossible over 40 mph. Because Richard Pope returned his

This Atlantic, when it was owned by Richard B. Pope, about 1940.

Atlantic for fitting of the supercharger to increase its performance, one might surmise that he spent most of his 37,500 miles in the car motoring in silence.

How many more resolutely sensational motorcars Jean Bugatti might have designed is tantalizing to conjure. But on a warm August evening in 1939 he took the streamlined Type 57G that had just won Le Mans on a final test before sending the car to the seaside resort of La Baule for the last competitive event of the season. Jean had accepted his father's dictum that he not race and compensated by driving very fast to assignations in Paris and testing the company's cars at all available opportunities. On this occasion Bugatti workmen blocked both ends of the Molsheim-Strasbourg road, and his younger brother Roland guarded the entrance to a little-used alley near the factory. As Jean sped down the road, a bicyclist brushed past Roland and onto the roadway. Jean swerved to avoid him, crashed and died at the age of thirty.

Jean's death haunted Ettore Bugatti, and just weeks after the accident, Europe erupted in war. Bugatti remained in Paris designing an airplane, modifying the Royale engine for marine application, and developing a 21-cubic-inch 12,000-rpm engine for use in a motorcycle or mini-car. The factory in Molsheim was confiscated by the Germans. Following the liberation of France, Bugatti went to court to reclaim his factory and lost the case. During spring 1947, while in Colmar seeing to his appeal, Bugatti asked his long-time chauffeur Toussaint to drive him to Molsheim in the Royale coupe that remained his car of choice. He looked longingly at the factory but was forbidden to go inside. Next he asked his chauffeur to take him to the spot where Jean had been killed. There he fell to the ground unconscious. Toussaint carried his boss to the Royale and drove him back to Paris. On June 11 the court gave him his factory back. Ettore Bugatti never knew it. He remained in a coma and died on August 21.

The company struggled on fitfully for a few years. After his father's death, Roland Bugatti said, "Le Patron est mort, la voiture est morte aussi." And it was true. The Bugatti automobile died with the man who created it.

— BRK

Jean Bugatti and a Type 35C between Molsheim and Mutzig, 1927.

1954 MORGAN PLUS FOUR

THE MORGAN is sublime because it is singular. And odd. This holds true for every Morgan ever built, from the first one that left the Malvern Link factory in Worcestershire in 1910 to the one that will leave tomorrow. The car remains hand built by what is now the oldest independently owned sports car manufactory in the world.

Loathness to change has ever been the company hallmark. The Morgan was born as a three-wheeler because building light and inexpensive was best achieved that way. A vehicle more than a motorcycle but not quite a car was also attractive in England for tax purposes. Henry Frederick Stanley Morgan exhorted the three-wheeler rationale with the fervor of a preacher. His father, the Reverend Prebendary H. G. Morgan, vicar of Stoke Lacey and financial angel behind the company, routinely dashed into print in defense of his son's trike. Success in motor sport competition drew a loyal, almost cultish following to the company's product for the next quarter century.

In 1936, in an event of almost epochal proportion, the Morgan was transformed from two cylinders and three wheels to four cylinders and four wheels, or the 4-4 as the factory differentiated it. H. F. S. saw that the revision was wrought with as little deviation from Morgan practice as possible. Twice the number of wheels in front might have suggested a change in suspension, but no, the trike's entire front-end structure, with independent front suspension by coil springs and sliding pillars, remained. "A system patented by the Morgan Motor Co. and used by them with every satisfaction" was

H. F. S. Morgan in 1913.

the official justification and remained so to the end of the century. "Next to a Morgan," H. F. S. liked to say, "a Rolls-Royce is as good a car as you can buy."

Peculiarly for Morgan, the 4-4 was reintroduced in 1946 as the 4/4. Perhaps this change happened because during those awful years when the factory was engaged in the war business, H. F. S. and his son Peter Morgan, who became managing director, forgot how the designation was written. The Plus Four arrived in 1950, the "four" this time representing the increase in wheelbase (from 92 to 96 inches). Following its debut at the London Motor Show at Earls Court in October, *The Motor* wrote admiringly that the Plus Four was "a small car with a larger engine in a wonderful all-round performance."

What was uniquely wonderful about the new car was how little it had changed from the 1936 design of the 4-4 cum 4/4. Its virtue was timelessness. Upright in profile, the Morgan Plus Four exuded character and verily shrieked its reluctance to capitulate to prevailing styling trends. The narrow, tapering and louvered hood, the swept fenders, and the set-apart headlights were design themes that most of the industry worldwide had begun to abandon at the time the 4-4 was originally introduced. The gentle curving of the radiator into the cowl was a nod to aerodynamics and streamlining but the radiator bars remained stoutly vertical and without the surround molding that other automakers thought necessary. There was little about a Morgan that bore direct comparison with conventional cars. What manufacturer would admit that his chassis was "whippy," as Peter Morgan did? What manufacturer other than this one would stoutly declare, "I don't mind if they say Morgans are for mad people"? The state of their sanity notwithstanding, drivers of a Mog, as their owners affectionately refer to the car, were probably as singular as their steed. Few would purposely buy an automobile that rattled one's teeth and shook one's bones on any surface other than smooth macadam. The Washington, D.C., chapter of the Morgan Owners Club proudly named its newsletter "The Roughrider."

Vintage in concept deserved vintage in execution, and Morgan did not disappoint. Although brush painting was discontinued shortly after World War II, one factory craftsman refused to pick up a spray gun and was allowed to brush paint until his retirement. Two decades after the car on these pages was built, Peter Morgan muttered that he might consider power tools but, for the time being, cutting body panels out with tin snips worked fine. The Morgan frame was Belgian ash; steel or aluminum coachwork was the buyer's choice.

Morgans like this one remained in "batch production," as the company termed its manufacturing method, for nearly two decades.

Disk brakes and safety equipment might be incorporated as time went on but creature comforts would never be part of the package. The Plus Eight became the new model in 1969 because Morgan's source for engines (Triumph) discontinued its four; Peter Morgan had to

Illustration of the first Morgan three-wheeler, drawn by John Black.

shop for a new one and bought Rover's V8. That car remained in production into the twenty-first century.

In a world that saw manufacturers pay almost universal obeisance to a school of design that produced jelly bean look-alike cars, it became pleasant to reflect upon the Morgan as documentary evidence that the automotive art can be artless, that an anachronism can be vastly entertaining. "The only possible reason for buying such a car," the *Motor* once remarked, "is the sheer fun of driving it fast on suitable roads."

A new century and a global world brought change, of course. Peter Morgan's son Charles, now managing director, had no choice but to succumb to reality. The all-aluminum Aero 8 of 2001, the first new Morgan model in sixty years, is no jelly bean but it is modern. The grille is the same. And although one may step over rather than on it, there is a running board. Best of all, the Morgan is still odd.

— BRK

1950 JAGUAR XK120 ALLOY ROADSTER

ASIGN ON THE WALL in the Jaguar design studios in Whitley, England, says simply, "A Jaguar is a copy of nothing." That is how Sir William Lyons wanted it. It often takes a single visionary to create an extraordinary automobile. Bugatti, Ferrari, and Porsche were all named after their founders. Aston Martin became *Aston Martin* because of the drive, determination, and vision of David Brown. With Jaguar, it was "Sir William."

William Lyons was born into a musical family in Blackpool in 1901, though the family profession doesn't seem to have affected his career choice. By the age of eighteen, he was apprenticing at Crossley Motors and taking engineering classes at night. He began his automotive career as a salesman but was soon making more money fixing and reselling war-surplus motorcycles. He also made sidecars, a profitable endeavor that led him to form the Swallow Sidecar Company in 1923 with William Walmsley. That trait—a willingness to gamble on what he felt was right—remained with Lyons throughout his career.

By 1928 the business had expanded to man-ufacturing special bodies for the mass-market Austin Seven. Later, Swallow Sidecars also made bodies for Fiat and Standard, among others, and so impressed Standard Motors's John Black that he signed an agreement with Lyons to produce a body for a special 6-cylinder model. The car was called the Standard Swallow, and Lyons moved Swallow Sidecars to a new facility in Coventry to handle the work.

The liaison with Standard was key to the formation of Jaguar. Standard agreed to supply Swallow with a chassis, and in 1931 Swallow showed its first car under its own name, the S.S.1. Its sensational looks demonstrated that Lyons understood the pulse of the market and had the ability to produce it at a bargain of a price. As Harold Pemberton remarked in the *Daily Press* in 1932, "Last year I described the S.S.1 as the car with the 1,000-pound look. This year it might be called the car with the 1,500-pound look. And it costs only 325 pounds."

In 1935 the company went public as SS Cars and Walmsley retired, leaving Lyons in complete control. It soon debuted its second model, which Lyons called the Jaguar, the name by which all his subsequent cars would be known.

The SS Jaguar 100 was nothing short of stunning, a stupendous-looking two-seat roadster with sweeping fenders, sparkling proportions, and a top speed of one hundred miles per hour, a very rare figure at the time. That set the tone for all subsequent Jaguars. Lyons's machines offered tremendous presence and performance at a cost that was substantially less than one would pay for the corresponding Bentley and, later, Ferrari or Maserati.

From the start Jaguar was Sir William's fiefdom, and for the next three decades and more he ruled it through intimidation. Taller than many of the people who worked for him, Lyons was a very formal man who looked like a banker in crisp pinstripe suits and pressed white shirts, topped with distinctive silver hair. He was a stickler for detail, and stories abound among the company's employees of production-line foremen sprinting to pick up a screw and place it in its bin because Sir William was on his way.

Lyons would look at any method possible to save money. Geoff Turner was an apprentice when he first met Sir William in the early 1960s. Turner and three or four other work-ers were heading over to make tea for their mid-morning break when they noticed Lyons and several other men approaching them. Asked where they thought they were going, Turner answered that it was break time. "No it isn't," was the stern reply. "There are thirty seconds to go. Stand there!" When the whistle sounded, Lyons said, "Go make your tea now."

But Turner came to appreciate Lyons while developing the revolutionary XJ6 sedan several years later, finding him abrupt but not sharp. "I always got the impression that his mind was turning over [so] fast that he didn't have the time to listen to the end of a sentence," he said. Sir William could also show unexpected fairness. One time in a paint booth, an employee accidentally hit him in the chest with a car door, knocking the "Old Man" to the floor. After Lyons was helped to his feet and had regained his breath, he turned to the cowering employee and said, "I do apologize. That was totally my fault. I should have realized you couldn't see me."

Because of such moments, Jaguar employees were willing to walk through fire to achieve what Lyons wanted. He was a man with a vision,

one his workers greatly respected and believed in. "He could draw on the back of a cigarette packet what he desired, and he expected you to produce it," said former employee Roy Pointer. "It was gut feeling with him." Most amazing was how many times that gut was right.

Jaguar vaulted onto the world spotlight in the fall of 1948. At the London Motor Show, the company wanted everyone to swoon over its new Mk V, a handsome but conservatively styled sedan aimed at America and other export markets.

But the car that dominated the headlines was the XK120 Roadster. Though Lyons would not likely have said it so bluntly, he understood that sex sells, and he designed the roadster for one reason: to showcase Jaguar's all new 6-cylinder engine powering the Mk V. This was one of the first twin overhead cam engines to be put into large-scale production, and its sophisticated configuration gave Jaguar cars considerably more power than if they had used traditional technology. Lyons had his men develop it because he wanted to anticipate what the competition would be doing ten years later. To make sure his employees didn't give up on the complex, arduous task, he insisted the engine enter production, and that was all it took to keep the troops fired up.

The XK120 and its memorable motor were nothing short of astonishing. "As a technical achievement," *Motor Trend*'s March 1950 cover story concluded, "the [XK120] is outstanding . . . It is evident that Jaguar Cars Ltd. has produced a car that will be honored and admired by motoring enthusiasts for many years to come." Just as impressive was the car's appearance. British designs were typically austere and formal. With the XK120, Lyons created a shape that was flamboyant, distinctive, rounded, and flowing. There was no unnecessary adornment, just a look of pure, efficient speed.

The car was an overnight sensation. Jaguar planned to make only two hundred to promote the new engine, but was immediately bombarded with orders, particularly from America —Jaguar's California importer said he would buy the entire production run. As ace English driver Sir Stirling Moss put it, "The XK120 made such an impact that everybody wanted one. But they were nearly all for export so you couldn't buy one for love nor money."

The clamor was especially great in southern California, the home of movie studios and image-conscious stars. Much in the way Ferrari's Spyder California (see pages 152–57) represents the optimism and good life found at the end of the 1950s, the XK120 makes the same statement about the early part of the decade. It may not be as chic and sleek as the Ferrari, but there is no doubt it is beautiful, a distinction that stood out from anything made at the time. Fittingly, Clark Gable took the first delivery of the first XK120 in the States. Others such as Humphrey Bogart would soon follow, and Jaguar's slinky roadster became an integral part of Hollywood life. Famed photographers such as Sid Avery often placed such stars as Bogart and Becall in or near their XK120 when taking portrait photos.

As the orders came in nonstop, Jaguar recognized the car's potential for racing. An XK120 would go 132 mph on a closed road in Belgium, a record for a production car when most everything else struggled to clear 80 mph. Still, Lyons was no fool, and he and his engineering

Sir William Lyons shares a relaxed moment with the legendary racing driver Tazio Nuvolari, Silverstone, 1950.

staff recognized the difference between cruising at high speed for several minutes down a straight versus several hours of accelerating, stopping, and cornering during a race.

Jaguar decided to enter competition at England's Silverstone race in 1949, but before agreeing with the organizers Lyons had his men flog one for three hours at the famed track to make sure they would not be embarrassed. His team was doing its best to break the car during that test when Lyons showed up, wanting to try the car himself.

As author Paul Skilleter notes, the episode became the stuff of legend. The company's public relations man Bill Rankin was in the passenger seat when Lyons slipped behind the wheel. He turned to a startled Rankin and announced that he didn't have his glasses with him, so would Rankin please tell him where

the corners and braking points were. And with that he floored the accelerator. Several laps later Lyons pulled in the pits grinning ear-to-ear, Rankin white as a sheet.

The XK120 was a successful racer, chalking up a victory at that initial outing at Silverstone. In 1950 chassis number 660043, the car shown here, competed in Italy's famed Mille Miglia. It finished eighth overall out of several hundred competitors. Three other XK120s competed two months later at Le Mans, the world's most famous race. One ran as high as second more than halfway through the twenty-four-hour classic, but retired later from mechanical problems. That episode and others made Jaguar aware that a purpose-built car—one designed specifically for competition—was necessary to take home the trophy.

—WSG

1955 JAGUAR XKD

A S A RESULT of its experience at Le Mans, Jaguar first developed the XK120C, or "C-Type." The car was created with one goal in mind, to win the race, and it did just that in 1951 and 1953, making Jaguar a well-known name outside England. But by 1953 the competition at Le Mans had become faster and tougher, and in response Jaguar created a replacement for the C-Type, which they logically baptized the D-Type.

Perhaps no car from the fifties represents speed better than this racing Jaguar. The tail on the rear is straight from a jet fighter. The front is rounded and smooth, a blunt instrument to cut the air. The headlights sit behind covers that sweep the air up over the fenders. The windshield is cut down lower than one would expect, and the wheels are tucked inside the car's clean fuselage of a body. Like its predecessor, the D-Type was made specifically to win. That the D-Type seemingly took many design cues from aircraft is appropriate, considering the construction of its chassis. High-performance and racing cars in the 1950s typically used a frame composed of numerous tubes, arranged at intricate angles for maximum rigidity. In contrast, the D-Type used a monocoque structure, making the aircraft analogy all the more appropriate.

A monocoque structure is a single sheet of aluminum or steel to which the suspension, engine, and other mechanics are attached at various points by brackets or some other method. The benefits are several: the strength-to-weight ratio is very high; it spreads the "loads" of components evenly throughout the structure; and it can sit very low to the ground. Nature offers a perfect example of the monocoque in the eggshell.

Because of the car's ultra-high performance potential, Lyons deferred its design to Malcolm Sayer, an aerodynamicist with a background in aviation. Whereas the C-Type had been created to resemble the XK120, the D-Type was designed from scratch. In the book *Jaguar Sports Racing Cars*, Sayer would describe his mandate as "functional efficiency at all costs."

Aircraft engineering principles were also used in the D-Type's dry-sump lubrication system. Typically an engine sits on top of the oil pan and then draws the oil up into it, which places the engine higher in the car. A dry sump system has an external container from which oil is then pumped to the engine. With no oil pan to worry about, Jaguar's men could lower

Mike Hawthorne and Ivor Bueb won Le Mans in 1955 in this long-nose D-type. It was the first of three successive D-type victories at the world's most famous and important race.

the engine that much farther. Coupled with the monocoque chassis, the D-Type's height was some thirty percent lower than the C-Type's, making the car more efficient aerodynamically and a much better handling machine.

The D-Type's first appearance came at Le Mans in 1954. The car cleared 170 mph down the long Mulsanne Straight—20 mph faster than the C-Type. One came in second to a Ferrari 375 Plus in a very close finish. But the following three years were an entirely different story, with the D-Type winning Le Mans each time.

The D-Type shown here, chassis XKD 505/601, was the first of the "long-nose" variety. The new, more aerodynamic configuration made the D-Type likely the fastest race car of the 1950s, able to clear 190 mph. XKD 505/601 finished second at Reims in 1956, then sixth at Le Mans in 1957.

Racing Jaguars such as the D-Type were typically painted a distinctive green color. In the 1950s and '60s, colors on racing cars represented specific countries: Jaguars were "British Racing Green," Ferraris were "*rosso corsa*" (competition red), French entries "French Blue," and with good reason—the car and the company were emblematic of the country from which it came. The war may have been over, but nationalist pride still ran very high.

Jaguar D-Type in the lead at the Goodwood Nine-Hour Race, 1955, driven by Bob Berry and Norman Dewis.

1957 JAGUAR XKSS

THERE IS AN OLD SAYING in automotive circles, "Win on Sunday, sell on Monday." Headlines of victory were particularly important in the 1950s and did much to promote the awareness of the Jaguar brand around the world. But there was another side to that axiom as well. A slightly de-tuned, more comfortable version of a race car appealed to sportsmen, amateur racers, and enthusiasts who wanted the fastest car available, and making it was an excellent way for a company such as Ferrari to amortize the costs of a competition program.

Jaguar's foray into that market was the XKSS. Demand for Jaguar production cars often exceeded supply, thanks to William Lyons's feel for his cars' tremendous combination of value and "Grace, Pace, Space," as the company's period advertisement so eloquently put it.

An exception to the "demand exceeding supply" rule was Jaguar's D-Type race car. Despite two Le Mans wins in a row, approximately thirty remained unsold in October 1956, when Jaguar announced its withdrawal from competition. The reasoning was simple: the D-Type was deemed to be obsolete, and this would allow the engineering department a year to create a successor. (In truth, the car was hardly outdated; privately entered D-Types would sweep the top four spots at Le Mans in 1957.)

Briggs Cunningham, an American sportsman who would greatly influence his country's road racing in the 1950s, was one of Jaguar's top customers in the States. Around the time of the withdrawal announcement he wanted a D-Type to race in events sanctioned by the Sports Car Club of America, but the SCCA would not accept the Jaguar as a production

Burned and damaged XKSS car bodies destroyed by the factory blaze of February 1957.

car. In order to qualify, the company had to produce at least fifty of the D-Type. So with a number of cars remaining in the factory, it was decided to convert them to a more comfortable "dual-purpose" car that was equally at home on the track or the street. The result, unveiled in January 1957, was the XKSS.

The prototype had been created from a design by Malcolm Sayer. He started with the D-Type, then made the windshield taller and gave it proper wraparound protection for the driver and passenger. The driving compartment was made roomier than the competition D-Type and had padded bucket seats, carpeting, and other comforts. Small doors were fitted and the rear wing or fairing behind the driver was removed and replaced by a luggage rack on the trunk. A canvas top, small bumpers, and turn-signal lights rounded out the exterior modifications, and William Lyons signed off on the new Jaguar.

The car went on sale in the U.S. at $7,500, or some $3,000 less than the Mercedes-Benz 300SL Roadster, its closest competitor in terms of price and road manners. And when it came to performance, the XKSS was in a league of its own, likely the world's quickest and fastest production car in 1957. Compared to the Mercedes, the Jaguar was faster (149 vs. 130 mph) and significantly quicker to 60 (5.2 vs. 7.0 seconds) and 100 (13.6 vs. 18.9). That type of performance, coupled with the Le Mans victories, made Jaguar *the* employer of choice in England's booming auto industry. "There was a type of buzz, working for Jaguar," said former employee Tony Burton. "Jaguar was that little bit elevated above everyone else, even more than Rolls-Royce."

The XKSS, though, contributed very little to that "buzz." As production was getting under way in February 1957, a fire broke out in the factory, destroying the wing where the XKSS production line was housed. Though the XKSS is collected like fine art today (only eighteen were ever made), the men who built them had other things on their minds at the time. Still, the company emerged from the calamity in even finer shape than before. The cars were better built after the fire, and there was certainly no dent in Jaguar's creativity or Sir William's insight into the market's desires. Four years later, Jaguar would unveil what many consider the greatest car of the 1960s: the E-Type.

—wsg

1954 FERRARI 375 PLUS

ORE THAN ANY OTHER postwar
manufacturer, Ferrari has a reputation for producing cars that are
viewed as art. The reason is simple: from 1950 into the mid-1970s,
Italy was the center of the automotive design
universe, and Ferrari was courted by the best
carrozzerie, the country's unparalleled automobile designers and body builders. "My father
may have been a very engine-oriented person," said Enzo Ferrari's son Piero, a vice president in the company, "but second was the
coachwork. The style was very important to
him. Every car, every prototype was supervised
by him personally. I remember many times my
father walking into the Scaglietti plant and
watching a prototype that wasn't painted,
something just sitting there in bare aluminum.
He would say, 'I don't like this radius here.
Make it bigger, make it sharper.'"

Enzo Ferrari was in his late fifties and
already a well-known personality in Italy and
the racing world when he began building his
dynamic cars in 1947. His burning desire to
construct fast machines under his own name
had started many years earlier and only grown
stronger during World War II. Born in 1898,
Ferrari was the youngest son of a well-to-do
metal-shop owner who lived near Modena, in
central Italy. At the age of ten he saw his first
race on the outskirts of Bologna. "The crowds
were all shouting for the Number 10 car, driven
by Felice Nazzaro, who won the race," Ferrari
observed in his memoirs. "My father and
brother were always talking about cars and I
got more and more interested as I listened to

their talk . . . It was watching races . . . being
close up to those cars and those heroes, being
part of the yelling crowd, that whole environment that aroused my first flicker of interest
in motor cars."

After his discharge from the military in 1918,
Ferrari entered the auto industry with a firm
that stripped truck bodies so the naked chassis could be used for cars. That job took him
to Milan where he frequented the Vittorio
Emanuele bar, an established hangout for racing drivers and others connected with the automotive world. Networking there got him a
job at CMN, a short-lived auto manufacturer
based in Milan, which in turn led to an open-
ing at Alfa Romeo in 1920. There, Ferrari
gained great notoriety as an astute organizer
and behind-the-scenes force. He remained
closely tied to Alfa Romeo until the late 1930s,
when he had an ugly breakup with the firm;
shortly afterward, he made two cars under the
name Auto Avio Costruzioni. During World

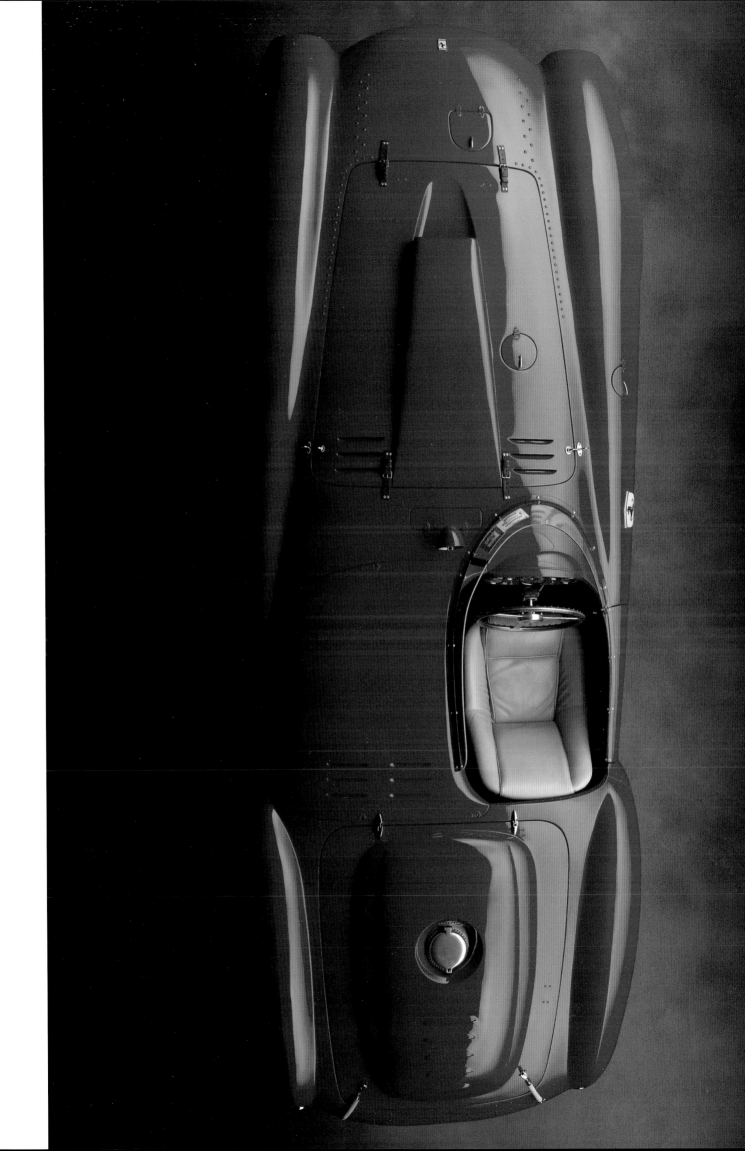

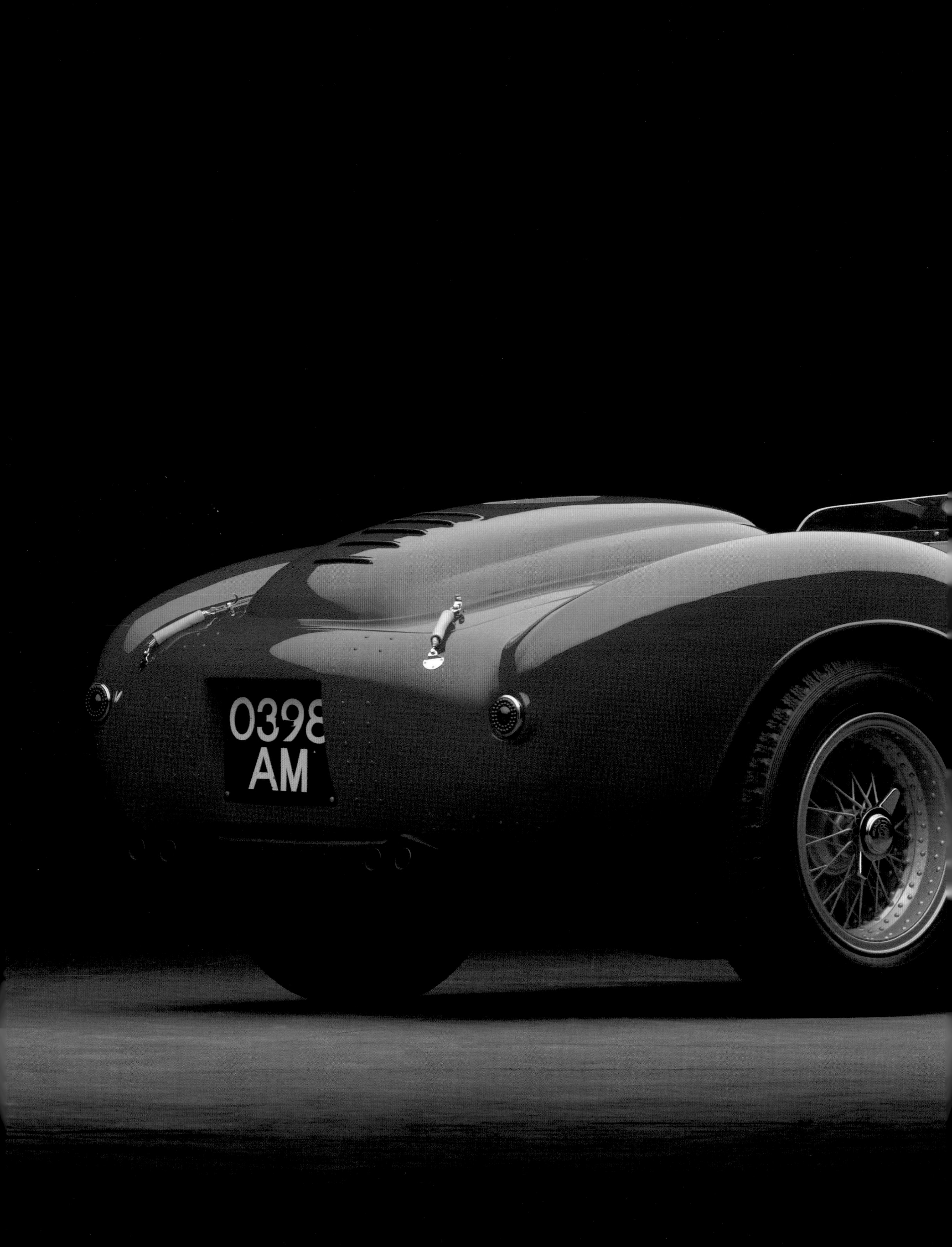
0398
AM

War II he ran a prosperous business manufacturing machine tools, but no sooner did hostilities end in May 1945 than he began eyeing a return to the front lines of competition.

Of particular importance was the car's "heart": The "Old Man," as Ferrari was affectionately known inside his company, felt it should have a 12-cylinder engine. He used every ounce of his charisma and contacts to overcome material and manpower shortages. His factory resided in Maranello, a small village outside Modena, a location that made a bad situation even worse. Roads were filled with craters, people had to rely on barges to cross the rivers because bombing had destroyed most bridges, and train service was spotty at best.

Still, supplies came in at a slow but steady pace, and Ferrari's first "car," if one can call it that, took its maiden voyage on March 12, 1947. The model was designated the 125 S, "125" referring to the capacity in cubic centimeters of an individual cylinder. One snapshot taken that day shows a proud Enzo Ferrari sitting in the running chassis, elegantly adorned in suit and tie and smiling at the camera. The car's body had yet to be built, and the exposed mechanicals were anything but beautiful—its tubular chassis, homely disc wheels, and small radiator had an appearance and finish far from the polished, impeccable sheen seen in today's production and racing Ferraris.

The company's first racing victory came nine weeks later at Rome. The car was a crude-looking machine with a cigar-shaped body and cycle fenders, nothing more than an evolution of the prewar designs seen on some of the Scuderia Ferrari's Alfa Romeos. But as Ferrari garnered more victories, coachbuilders such as Allemano began building bodies for him, giving the handful of machines a variety of looks. This troubled Enzo's keen marketing instincts—a nonuniform look did not promote Ferrari as a "brand."

He turned to Carrozzeria Touring, one of Italy's two most prominent coachbuilding firms, for the solution. "Ferrari wanted to be recognized as a true motorcar constructor," said Carlo Anderloni, who took over the company's design department after the unexpected death of his father. "He wanted a distinctive, uniform appearance so that when someone saw one of his cars, they said, 'That is a Ferrari.'"

The resulting 166 *barchetta* Anderloni designed did just that. When four of them lined up at the 1949 Mille Miglia, the point was clear: Ferrari was a proper manufacturer, not some small constructor randomly creating machines like many of his competitors.

Touring-bodied Ferraris won the Mille Miglia, Le Mans, and a host of other races, the resulting publicity boosting Ferrari's prestige and sales in Italy and abroad. This caused other coachbuilders such Vignale, Ghia, and Zagato to clamor to make bodies for Ferrari, much like today's fashion designers yearn to have movie stars wear their latest styles at awards ceremonies. In 1952 a new coachbuilder entered the fray for Ferrari's business, one whose name would become synonymous with the company.

Then in his late fifties, Battista "Pinin" Farina was almost as famous as Ferrari in the auto industry (his name officially became Pininfarina in 1961). The tenth of eleven children, he was born just outside Turin; the nickname "Pinin" meant "baby of the family" in the local Piemonte dialect. His poverty-stricken family moved to the industrial city when Pinin was five due to his mother's steely determination and willingness to gamble—a trait her son would inherit.

Pinin entered the coachbuilding trade in 1905 at the age of twelve, when his brother Giovanni opened Stablimenti Industriali Farina S.A., a body repair shop that also made seats for racing drivers. Five years later the company moved to larger premises and began designing and constructing new car bodies. As Pinin's own design skills had increased tremendously, he was put in charge of several departments. He also dealt comfortably with wealthy and powerful clients, and in 1920 he traveled to America to study advanced construction techniques.

Even more than his brother, Pinin was blessed with an innate talent and had the eye

to exploit it. "He was a very good technician who had good intuition of aerodynamics," says his son Sergio. "He was a master of forms, with very good taste and a great sense of balance." Using these skills, he formed Carrozzeria Pininfarina in 1930, and by the beginning of World War II the company was second only to Carrozzeria Touring in Italy in terms of prestige. Throughout the war Pinin's mind never stopped contemplating numerous shapes, trying new ideas and forms. Once hostilities ended, that constant dreaming became reality, yielding an uninterrupted stream of cars that were breathtakingly beautiful and often boldly experimental.

Pinin was expanding his horizons when he began courting Enzo Ferrari in the early 1950s. The two men had watched each other's careers with admiration. "It was [Ferrari's] character that interested me, as tightly closed as a walnut, disdaining the bonds the world proffered," Pinin observed in his autobiography. "It was obvious that for some time he was looking for his 'own' coachbuilder with whom he could establish a new kind of harmony." As for Ferrari, he noted in his own memoirs that he "had dealings with some of the greatest names in the business . . . all of them eager to build bodies for our cars. What I wanted for my cars was character and I found that with the help of Giovanni Battista Pininfarina."

Enzo Ferrari (center), in the Ferrari pit at Monza, smiles at remarks from Italian driver Alberto Ascari (left) while British driver Mike Hawthorn reads the racing news in English, September 1953.

The winning Ferrari 375 Plus in the pit at Le Mans, 1954.

Enzo Ferrari chats with Alfred Neubauer of Mercedes-Benz before the Italian Grand Prix in Monza, 1953. Ferrari was thought to be considering retirement after a series of accidents caused the deaths of four of his best drivers, but following a narrow defeat at Monza, he made it clear he would continue racing.

By this time, Ferrari was becoming more and more provincial and leaving Modena less and less often; those who wanted to do business went to him. Unfortunately, Pinin felt the same way. "Both men were prima donnas," Sergio Pininfarina said. "Ferrari was a man of very strong character, and my father was much the same. My father was *not* going to Modena, and Mr. Ferrari was *not* coming to Turin. So in the end they met halfway in the town of Tortona, something like Gorbachev and Reagan agreeing to meet in Iceland in the 1980s."

Pinin handed the account off to Sergio after that luncheon meeting, and the resulting relationship between Sergio, his father, their company's design department, and Enzo Ferrari is unlike any other in auto history. For the past five decades and more, Pininfarina has designed the vast majority of Ferrari's street cars, making one breathtaking, coveted creation after another.

Though Carrozzeria Pininfarina is noted for its work on Enzo's road cars, it is appropriate that the Lauren collection's earliest Ferrari is the visceral yet sensual 375 Plus, for Ferrari existed, and still exists, to compete. "No matter what formula, we have to race," said Piero Ferrari. "To race is like to be alive . . . and in our early years endurance racing was really part of the Ferrari myth, and was what built up the Ferrari myth in that age."

Pininfarina was a large contributor to that mystique. In 1953 the company began designing and constructing competition machines that featured rounded, flowing bodies accentuated by a long hood and graceful back in the never-ending search for greater aerodynamic efficiency.

One of the most majestic competition cars was the 375MM, built as both a *berlinetta* (fastback) and open-air spyder (the term commonly used for an Italian-made roadster). Everything was done to save weight and enhance performance, from using the thinnest gauge aluminum possible to making the windows in plastic rather than glass. The car won the championship that year, beating England's Jaguar. But Ferrari wanted to increase the performance still further, and so from the 375MM he developed the 375 Plus, using an approach that was common in America: he enlarged the engine to gain more power. Pininfarina and his men made the necessary modifications to the design.

One of the reasons for the *carrozzeria*'s success was that Pinin's men were true magicians with metal, able to make beautifully rounded forms by hand. As metalworker Ugo Bassano related, there were no blueprints for the designs. Pinin imagined the car in his mind, and they would make it with hammers and tongs, following his instructions in local dialect. Often the instructions were minute, shaving a little here, adding a little "oomph" there. "You would just pray you understood," Bassano said. "And until you really had understood, you would just have to do it over and over again."

Pininfarina worked flat out to meet the demands of clients such as Ferrari. All involved knew the deadline they were up against—the next race. And so it was with the 375 Plus. An absolute stunner in appearance, it proved to be incredibly reliable and fast. In 1954 it won two of the world's greatest races, Le Mans and the multi-day Carrera Panamericana in Mexico, and helped Ferrari secure another world championship.

—WSG

1958 FERRARI 250 TESTA ROSSA

ANOTHER COACHBUILDER who struck Enzo Ferrari's fancy in the 1950s was Modena resident Sergio Scaglietti. His is a true rags-to-riches story, one that would play an instrumental role in several of Ferrari's world championship cars.

Scaglietti was born in January 1920, the youngest of six children. His father was a master carpenter residing in Modena, a profession that left him hard pressed to pay the bills. Sergio recalls stealing a farmer's fruit for snacks and needing five months to earn enough money to buy a bicycle. Modena's damp, foggy winters were just tolerable because for half the year he worked at a business where there was a furnace.

Scaglietti's schooling was cut short in February 1933 when his father unexpectedly died. "That was a real trauma for the family," he remembers. "At that time, my brothers all had jobs. Three of them followed in my father's footsteps and were carpenters. My eldest brother and I were the only ones to choose a different path." That path began at age thirteen, when Sergio joined his brother at Carrozzeria Emiliana, a small auto repair shop near a canal. Such a calling was natural for the young Scaglietti: for as long as he could re-

member he relished working with his hands, turning pieces of metal into proper forms.

Carrozzeria Emiliana proved to be the perfect school for this, and more. What fascinated him was the covering of a car being made or repaired. The men typically created a series of tubes and placed them over the chassis to portray the lines of the car's body. Once the "frame" was completed they would make the body panels based on the frame's form.

In 1937 Sergio left Carrozzeria Emiliana when his brother and Renato Torcelli formed Carrozzeria Torcelli & Scaglietti. Their location couldn't have been better: directly across the street was the Scuderia Ferrari. The new company was soon repairing body panels on the Scuderia's Alfa Romeos.

When Italy entered World War II in 1940, Scaglietti and his brother were too old for the draft, and during the war years they repaired the handful of small vans and cars that were on the roads. After peace was declared, Scaglietti's skills were in constant demand to make and repair boats, reconstruct bridges, and refurbish the occasional car.

By the 1950s Scaglietti was again repairing cars full-time. Ferrari was by now producing two or three cars a month, and it was inevitable

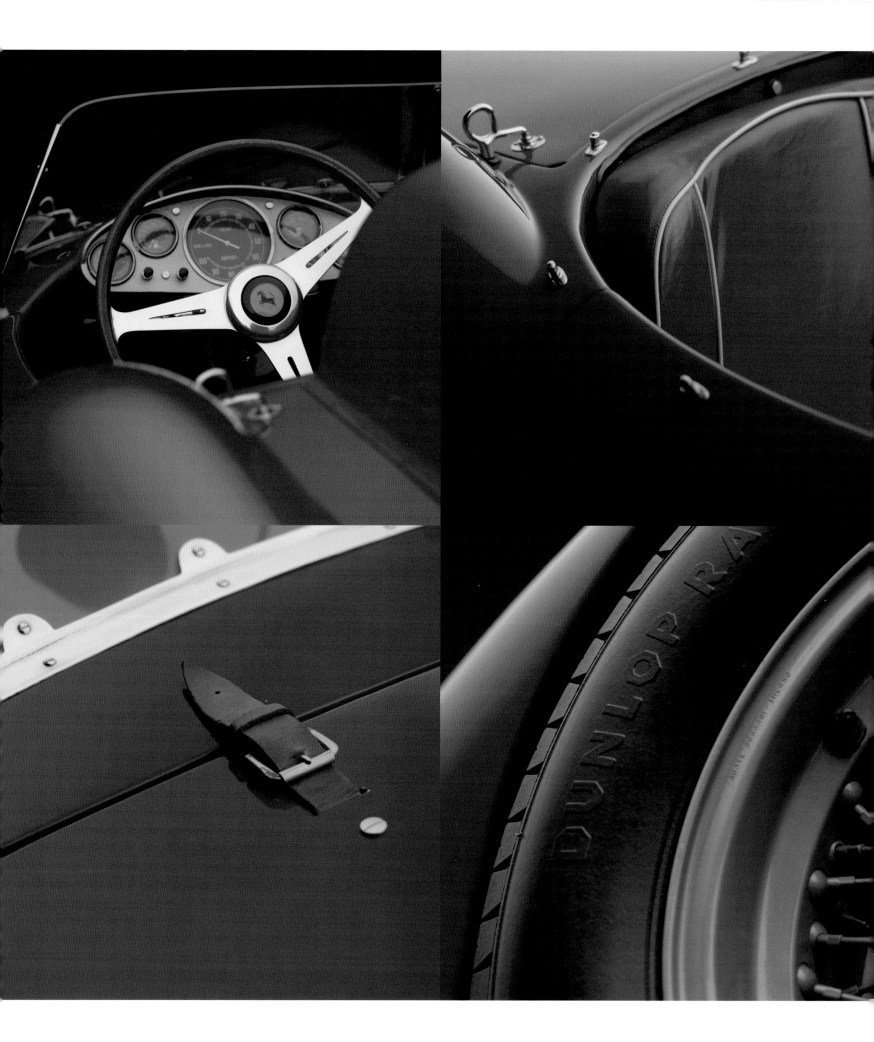

that the two men's paths would cross. The cat-
alyst was Alberico Cacciari, a gentleman racer
from Bologna, who approached Scaglietti to
create an entirely new body for his crashed
Ferrari. Enzo Ferrari later saw it, liked it, and
began sending work to the young coachbuilder.
Ferrari had another reason to like Scaglietti as
well. Enzo's son Dino was passionate about his
father's work, but a serious health condition
(most likely muscular dystrophy) left him un-
able to keep up with the pace of the Ferrari factory. Scaglietti's small body shop, located near
the Ferrari household, became Dino's second
home, and Ferrari appreciated the kindness
and respect with which Sergio treated his son.

By 1954 Scaglietti was a "sanctioned" Ferrari
coachbuilder, receiving bare chassis directly
from the maker. That year he designed and constructed bodies on Ferrari's competition models, the 500 Mondial and 250 and 750 Monzas.

Though Sergio was never formally trained
in the art of being a stylist, Ferrari trusted his
innate ability. Scaglietti relied on his teenage
memories, recalling the craftsmen's thin metal
tubes to determine a car's shape. Using the
technique, he instructed his men on the car's
general design, and they would make the tube
frame to put over the chassis. The process normally took three days, and once the design met
Scaglietti's approval, the body panels would be
shaped by beating them against a wooden buck
or sand-filled canvas bag.

Unlike virtually every other coachbuilder,
Scaglietti never put pen to paper to sketch a
design. He did everything "by the eyes alone,"
saying "good taste, aerodynamics, style, and
function" were the main elements of his designs. In 1957 and 1958 the last three ingredi-
ents came together to create a true Scaglietti
masterpiece, the 250 Testa Rossa. In Italian
the evocative name means "red head," referring to the red color of the V12 engine's cylinder heads. The engine displaced three liters
(twelve cylinders of 250 cc), and its roots can

be traced back to Ferrari's original V12, designed in the summer of 1945. Through continual experimentation in competition, the engine's power output increased along with its reliability, and by the mid-1950s it was rare to hear of Ferrari's 250 models not finishing races because of engine failure.

Scaglietti's first experience with a 3-liter V12 had been with the 250 Monza in 1954, which already featured some of his signature traits: long, flowing body, sensual covered headlights, and a headrest behind the driver. In 1956 the shape became even more stunning when Scaglietti created the coachwork for Ferrari's first Testa Rossa, the 500 TR, a favorite of racers in the U.S. and Europe. But it was the 250 TR that put the words "Testa Rossa" into the minds of racing enthusiasts everywhere, due to its world championship speed and Sergio's unforgettable coachwork.

The car's memorable shape was based on the design of Formula One racers, single-seat cars that normally had a torpedo-like body with pods on the sides. Scaglietti used a similar idea, designing the car's coachwork to bring air in toward the brakes to cool them.

Just how Scaglietti and his men calculated the height of the fenders demonstrates the truly hand built, seat-of-the-pants nature of the cars. "The suspension traveled about twenty centimeters," he said, "so to replicate its move-

ment we took old paint cans and put them on the wheels! The idea actually worked quite well." Scaglietti compared the technique to the precision found in today's electronically measured world. His eye was "good" to about one centimeter, meaning his creations often had a fender that was one centimeter higher than the other. Such tolerances, he muses, would be completely unacceptable today.

The prototype Testa Rossa standing in front of the pits before the start of the Twenty-four Hours of Le Mans, June 1959. By this time, this first model was no longer competitive and soon retired from the race with a broken gearbox.

Ferrari 250 Testa Rossa at the 1958 Le Mans, piloted by Ed Hugus and Ernie Erickson.

The TR has Scaglietti's signature headrest behind the driver, a styling element suggested several years earlier by Dino Ferrari. In 1954 Scaglietti had several Pininfarina-bodied 375s in the shop. Since their potent V12 engines required large gas tanks, the car's rear had several plateaus that looked like steps to make more room. Dino in particular didn't like this treatment, so Scaglietti created a new rear that tapered into a headrest behind the driver, a decision both the craftsman and Dino thought would improve aerodynamics. Enzo Ferrari, however, was furious when he saw the modification and demanded to know who changed the cars. Scaglietti confessed and offered to remove the headrests. But no sooner had he completed the work than Dino came into the shop, became furious in turn, and confronted his father. A sheepish Enzo Ferrari finally told Scaglietti that the headrests could stay. They would be used into the early 1960s on all open-competition Ferraris.

In 1958, at the season's first race in Buenos Aires, 250 TRs took three of the top four positions. They subsequently dominated the season, winning at Sebring in Florida, the Targa Florio in Sicily, and, most important, Le Mans. Ferrari handily won the world championship, having doubled the points of second- and third-place finishers Porsche and Aston Martin.

Just as enduring as that championship was the appearance of the car that won it. "The 250 Testa Rossa is my favorite creation from the period," Scaglietti says. "It was beautiful, for I would see different characteristics whenever I looked at it." Today it remains just as hypnotic as when the craftsmen's hands first took a hammer to the metal some five decades ago. —WSG

1961 FERRARI 250 TR 61 SPYDER FANTUZZI

ODAY THE PROSPEROUS central Italian city of Modena is widely recognized as the "Silicon Valley of Speed," home to Ferrari and many of the world's most prestigious automotive makers. The rural town's association with cars and performance began in the early 1930s, when Enzo Ferrari opened the Scuderia Ferrari; several years later Maserati's operations also moved to Modena. But the town's transformation into the world's performance mecca truly began in earnest in the 1950s. With the downsizing of Italy's aircraft industry after the war, a large number of talented engineers, machinists, and craftsmen needed jobs, and they found them in Modena's expanding auto industry. Much of what they knew passed through to the companies' street and racing cars. Engines became more powerful, and suspension, brakes, and chassis improved.

Thanks to the postwar "economic miracle" (see page 152), Ferrari's and Maserati's production increased more than one thousand percent in the 1950s, causing Modena, its constructors, and their glamorous offerings to jump into the jet set limelight and stay there. The resulting publicity drew numerous people to Modena and influenced Modenese residents to enter the industry.

One resident was Medardo Fantuzzi. A heavyset man who had a way with metal and a hammer, Fantuzzi was born in 1908 and entered the auto industry in 1924 as an apprentice with Maserati, where he stayed for the next two decades. He moved to Modena in 1940 to oversee production of Maserati's competition car bodies. In the early 1950s he started his own *carrozzeria*, located inside the Maserati works. The company was his only client, and through much of the decade he built nearly all the bodies for Maserati's sports racing and Formula One cars. The relationship lasted until the end of 1957, when Maserati withdrew from competition. Given his impressive reputation, it didn't take Fantuzzi long to move his coach-building shop under the Ferrari umbrella. He and his men would subsequently make many of Ferrari's most famous racing and Formula One bodies.

Some of the best-known cars were the later model Testa Rossas. Even before the end of the 1958 season, Ferrari began experimenting with the 250 TR for the following year. One idea was to modify Scaglietti's 250 TR "pontoon fender" coachwork. Pinin Farina made a prototype, then manufacture of the cars was entrusted to

Carlo Abate braking hard at the Guards International Trophy Race, August 1963, after losing a wheel. Later, this same 250 TR 61 became Count Giovanni Volpi's personal town car, and could sometimes be seen parked in front of the Hôtel de Paris in Monte Carlo.

Carrozzeria Fantuzzi, as Scaglietti had his hands full building the 250 Spyder California and 250 SWB.

Fantuzzi continued making the Testa Rossa's coachwork in 1960, then made two more in 1961; one of these was chassis 0780, the car shown here. Its first race was the 12 Hours of Sebring less than two months after its completion that January. Driving it were American Phil Hill and Belgium's Olivier Gendebien, the era's true ace endurance-racing duo. They finished first overall.

Later that year the same Testa Rossa was sold to Count Giovanni Volpi di Misurata, known today as the man behind the Venice Film Festival. Then just twenty-four, the Count was the only son of Giuseppe Volpi, one of Italy's most notable politicians and financiers. When his father passed away, young Giovanni inherited his immense fortune. That inheritance made him the perfect individual to become a patron of the arts. But rather than backing a painter or sculptor, his money supported the men who built cars by hand, especially racing cars.

His motivation, he says, was "the fun, the glory and the panache. Everything was much more reachable compared to today. Now it is like a war, with exponentially rising costs. Back then, it was like a duel." Adding spice to the recipe was his perception that Ferrari didn't like his clients to do well, which gave the whole episode "a little bit of pep." That became particularly true in 1962. Volpi was the patron behind the Scuderia Serenissima, a successful racing team that competed on the endurance circuit. He used many of the era's top drivers and preferred the best cars, making him one of Ferrari's largest clients.

But that all changed at the end of 1961 with the infamous "walkout," a massive firing of engineers and executives from Ferrari (see page 122). Sports and *gran turismo* cars had been a growth industry throughout the 1950s, so the ex-Ferrari renegades banded together to form a new company, ATS. Their idea was to challenge Ferrari on both the street and the racetrack, and one of their main backers was none other than Giovanni Volpi. The Count

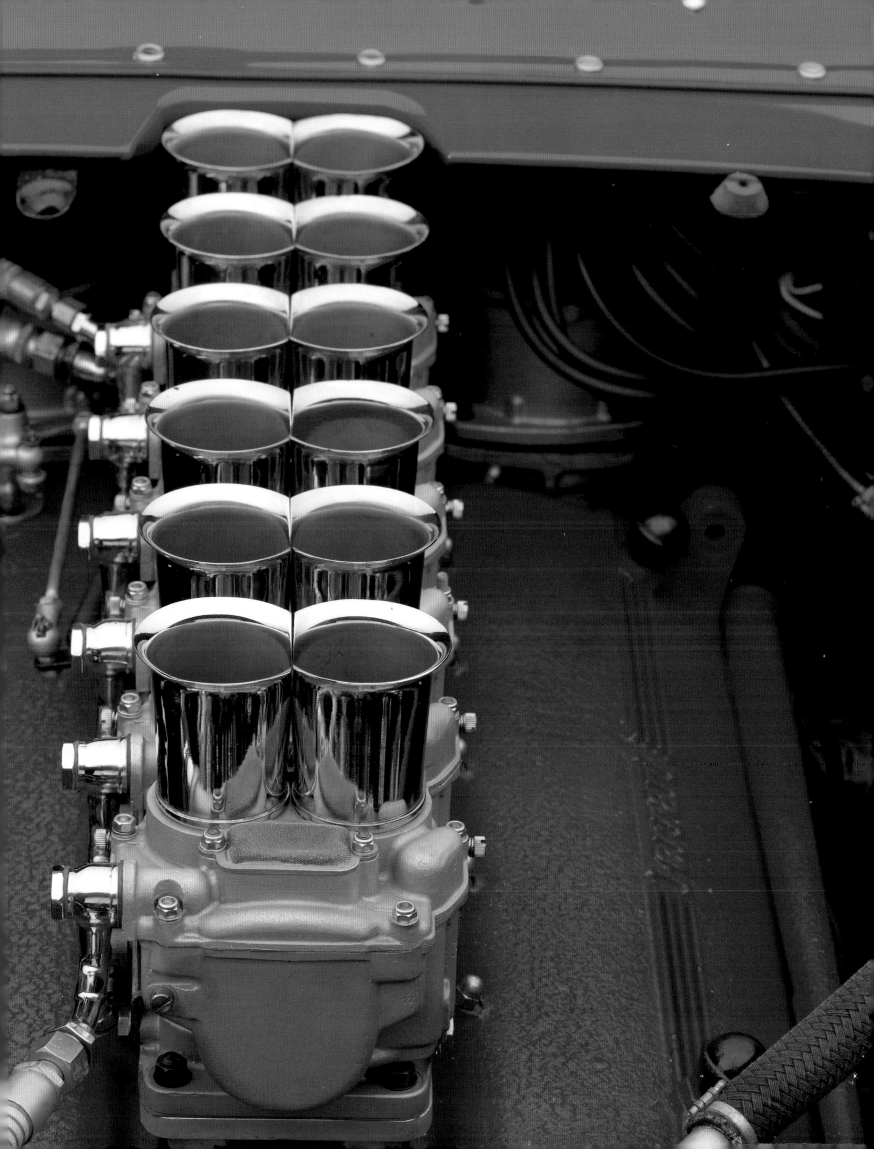

PROVA MO 74

was slated to get the first two GTOs, Ferrari's newest endurance racer, but when Enzo Ferrari learned of his involvement with ATS, the order was canceled.

Volpi, however, had a secret weapon in engineer Giotto Bizzarrini. Widely acknowledged as the father of the GTO, Bizzarrini had been one of the key people to leave Ferrari. With the 1962 season just around the corner, Volpi gave Bizzarrini a free hand with his recently acquired Testa Rossa. The engineer moved the engine back twelve centimeters and altered the suspension to make the car handle better.

The Count threw down the gauntlet at Sebring, his car proudly wearing the Scuderia Serenissima flag on its sides. Piloting it were Swedish driver Joakim Bonnier, a second-tier Formula One driver who did well in endurance races, and Italian Lucien Bianchi, an established long-distance driver. And much to Ferrari's chagrin, Volpi's Testa Rossa won the race.

The prevailing wisdom in automotive circles says that nothing is worse than last year's race car, but the TR's career was far from over. Late in 1962 Volpi had the coachwork altered, placing a horizontal spoiler just behind the cockpit, and lowered the tail's height. The car competed quite successfully in the 1963 season, finishing third overall in Germany's grueling thousand-kilometer race at the Nürburgring and first overall at Reims in France. It then retired from competition.

Volpi would continue to dabble in cars into the late 1960s, building a series of single-issue street and competition cars under the name Serenissima. They were stunning to look at, but the Count never again achieved the success he had enjoyed in the early 1960s with cars such as Testa Rossa 0780.

— w s g

1962 FERRARI 250 GTO

IN EARLY 1962 the Ferrari organization underwent a dramatic upheaval, one that would thrust artisan Sergio Scaglietti back into the limelight to create another sensational shape on a world-beating endurance racer. But unlike 1958's 250 TR, the 250 GTO was not the product of carefully planned execution. In March 1961 Ferrari's sales manager Girolamo Gardini returned from the Geneva Auto Show clearly shaken: Jaguar had just unveiled its E-Type coupe. Ferrari intended to use its 250 SWB model (see pages 146–51) to defend its title, but Gardini was convinced that the new Jaguar would beat them. A sense of urgency soon gripped the Ferrari organization. To prepare for the upcoming battle, Ferrari turned to engineer Giotto Bizzarrini.

Then thirty-five, Bizzarrini was the company's Controller of Experimental, Sports and GT Car Development, a lofty title for an extremely skilled test driver who happened to have an engineering degree. He had joined Ferrari in 1957 after three years at Alfa Romeo, and harbored a love of aerodynamics. His specialty was providing insightful, detailed engineering analysis from behind the wheel. This gave him abilities possessed by very few others—he could prove his ideas on both the drawing board and the road. "I became a test driver who happened to be an engineer who used mathematical principles," he observed. "For instance, if there is a crack in the wall, the mason comes in and patches it up. As an engineer, I would act almost like an architect, trying to figure out why the wall cracked. This is what I did during testing—anticipate or try to make the wall crack, pinpoint why it cracked, then offer the solution."

Ferrari ordered Bizzarrini to construct a new car, the first to be totally designed and built by the Experimental Department. This included even the body—a surprise, since the engineer was well aware of Scaglietti's role in manufacturing most of Ferrari's competition cars. And Bizzarrini recalls another unusual mandate: no one inside or outside the factory was to know of the new car's development. To ensure secrecy, he hand-picked four workers, then hired a bodyman from outside the Ferrari/Scaglietti circle.

Bizzarrini used a 250 SWB, a model he had helped develop, as his starting point. He then placed the entire engine behind the front axle. This improved the prototype's center of gravity for better handling and allowed him to create a new, lower, more aerodynamic hood line. Finally, he made a steeply raked windshield out of two pieces of glass that were joined in the center by a piece of aluminum. A crudely hand-formed fastback brought up the rear.

The prototype's creation saw an intense period of trial and error. Ferrari was present every day, keeping tabs on progress, hurrying his men along. Bizzarrini's group worked twenty-four hours a day, overtaken by the challenge and excitement of their task. Midnight phone calls were more the rule than the exception, the voice on the other end of the line saying, "*Ingegnere*, the car is ready for testing." A haggard Bizzarrini would then climb out of bed and, regardless of hour or weather, go out and complete another series of tests. Finally, in September 1961, the challenge thrown down by Ferrari saw results. At the prototype's first test at the Monza racetrack near Milan, racing drivers Stirling Moss and Willy Mairesse consistently turned laps several seconds faster than the 250 SWB.

Just as Bizzarrini prepared for further development testing, in the blink of an eye a new captain inherited the GTO helm. He, chief engineer Carlo Chiti, sales manager Girolamo Gardini, team manager Romolo Tavoni, and a handful of others suddenly found themselves on the outside of the company looking in, all casualties of November's infamous "walkout" or "palace revolt."

The event has been shrouded in mystery, but it is now clear that a longstanding series of clashes between Ferrari's wife, Laura, and Gardini lay at the upheaval's center. The company sales manager had finally had enough in late 1961, and after one particularly nasty altercation he headed to the restaurant where Ferrari was dining. There, the two had an explosive confrontation, and Gardini laid down an ultimatum: Get your wife under control. If

you don't, either she goes or I go. Ferrari's response was simply, "You're gone."

This abrupt event caught everyone off guard. But in every moment of crisis there is opportunity, and two who rose to the occasion were Sergio Scaglietti and Mauro Forghieri. Then in his late twenties, Forghieri was one of the few engineers remaining in Ferrari. The "Old Man" offered him the position of the racing department's chief engineer. This gave Forghieri the confidence necessary to focus on the task at hand. The faithful Scaglietti was entrusted with the GTO's bodywork, and he quickly decided to start from scratch. He found Bizzarrini's car too complicated, using too many tubes in its construction. Wanting to make something simple and easy to construct, he created, in his words, "a completely new car." Still, there are similarities between Bizzarrini's trial-and-error prototype and Scaglietti's version. Though the latter's is much more aesthetically pleasing, the general forms, proportions, and surface development show a family resemblance.

Like Bizzarrini, Scaglietti *had* to perform—he recalls constructing the car in twenty days. Making the difficult task even worse was a new regulation regarding windshield dimensions that forced them to alter the car's roofline while they were already constructing the body.

Back at Ferrari, Forghieri's development program started with a bang—literally! One

The setting looks still, but Graham Hill is driving this 250 GTO during the 1963 Tourist Trophy at well over 100 mph.

day Willy Mairesse tried the GTO prototype on a new highway between Bologna and Florence. Traffic was minimal and speed limits nonexistent, so Mairesse was soon blasting through the road's numerous curves and straights. But after exiting a tunnel and crossing a bridge, the Ferrari skidded off the road. Talking with Mairesse afterward, Forghieri concluded that the problems lay in the car's aerodynamics and set-up. Testing then moved to the Monza racetrack, where driver Lorenzo Bandini gave Forghieri an earful about the car's handling and stability.

Forghieri returned to the Ferrari factory to tackle the problems. Soon afterward, the 250 GTO and the rest of Ferrari's competition arsenal met the world's media in the factory's courtyard. America's *Road & Track* summarized the feelings of many: "The new Ferrari V-12 Gran Turismo coupe is a wild and woolly no-nonsense racing car . . . The new GT body is one of the most attractive, and at the same time most functional, yet seen on a competition car."

Those reviews hid the behind-the-scenes headaches of unresolved aerodynamics. Between the GTO's late February coming-out party and its racing debut in America one month later, Forghieri and crew tried a solution used on Ferrari's 1961 endurance racers: they added a small spoiler to the rear of the trunk. In testing, the results were immediate and dramatic. "Bandini was as quick as Stirling Moss," Forghieri smiles, "offering incisive proof the car was totally set up."

Two weeks later, at the Twelve Hour Race in Sebring, Florida, a GTO placed second overall and first in class, and the famed endurance racer went on to become one of the most legendary automobiles. Chassis 3987 GT, the GTO shown here, played a large role in that legacy. It entered four races in 1962 and won three. The following year it placed in the top ten in every race in which it competed, and finished second overall at Daytona behind another GTO.

When Scaglietti reflected on his creations, such as the 250 TR and GTO, he said he never tried to make revolutionary jumps with his designs, preferring each to be an evolution of those before it. Today his cars are often viewed as sculpture, but their creator claimed he never took time to step back and admire his work when it was new. "The reason was simple. We always had more work to do!"

—WSG

1955 PORSCHE 550 SPYDER

THE PORSCHE was born in a converted sawmill in the peaceful pastoral village of Gmünd at the foot of the Reisseck Mountains in Austria. Modest origins are tailor-made for legend making, but the name Porsche was poised at mythic status already. As creator of the K and S series Mercedes touring and sports cars, the thundering Auto Union Grand Prix racers and the People's Car (Volkswagen) for Adolf Hitler, Ferdinand Porsche's place in automobile history was secure well before he and his son Ferry left Germany for Austria in late 1944, taking plans for a sports car based on the Volkswagen with them. As Karl Ludvigsen subtitled his landmark book on the marque, "Excellence Was Expected."

By 1949 the Porsches had returned to the Zuffenhausen district of Stuttgart although not to their prewar design offices then in use by the U.S. Army occupying forces. Instead a workshop of 500 square meters was rented at Karosserie Reutter, the coachbuilding com-

pany contracted to produce the Porsche bodies and assemble the cars. With high hopes and royalties from the Volkswagen (now in production in Wolfsburg), the Porsches pursued the expected excellence. Engineering was the sole focus of father and son, which Ferry carried forward following the death of the senior Porsche in 1951.

Over the next half century, the Porsche's technical virtuosity would so overpower its persona that automobile magazine reviewers routinely expended rapturous pages of prose about the ingenuity of what the Porsche did so expertly without alluding to how the car looked doing it. Not until museums recognized the sculpting of the Porsche as a work of art did such scribes glance at the car long enough to reflect upon another of its virtues.

There is something cerebral about its look. The car emanates intelligence and a classic timelessness but, like a flapper's dress, the design is also both brief and very (there is no other word for it) cute. It is a clever and comely schizophrenia. Americans regarded the car warily at first. To some, it was a toy with a luxury automobile price. To the newly converted, it was a work of genius.

Ferdinand Porsche behind the wheel of one of his creations, January 1948.

That competition improved the breed had been the Porsche dictum since its genesis in Gmünd. The company's own entries and the *Eigenbau* (homemade) specials of Porsche friend Walter Glöckler, the VW distributor in Frankfurt, saw to the task early on, but by the fifties, modified production cars no longer were winning races and the company was persuaded to create one specifically for competition. Ninety such cars would be delivered, each weighing 1,500 pounds and displacing 1500 ccs by the addition of twin-choke Solex 40 PII downdraft carburetors to an already remarkable specification of an air-cooled horizontally opposed 4-cylinder engine combining

gear- and shaft-driven double overhead camshafts, roller-bearing crankshaft, and twin ignition. Suffice to say, Porsche got back to winning races.

Sanction for racing had mandated production of more cars than the factory could use itself, which provided "Potent Porsches," as the British *Autocar* put it, for the company to sell to enthusiasts. What to sell them as was a short-lived issue. At the Paris Automobile Salon in October 1953, Porsche referred to the prototype as 550/1500RS (respectively the type number, engine capacity, and *Renn Sport*, or "sports racing"). Impossible, U.S. importer Max Hoffman said, a name would be far more mar-

ketable. Heads put together arrived at "Spyder," the Italian term for a light two-seater body in a competition sports car, which of course perfectly described the new Porsche.

The 550 Spyder was so easy to drive fast that one road tester suggested beginners "might do well to stay in constant contact with the speedometer." On three continents, it demonstrated that the small manufacturing house of Porsche was very serious about racing. Factory-class victories at Le Mans in France, Sebring in Florida, the Carrera Panamericana in Mexico, and the 1,000 Kilometers of Buenos-Aires were paired with competition credits put up by Porsche 550 owners everywhere. In the U.S., Johnny von Neumann led a spirited group of Spyder drivers that won 1500-cc class events with maddening predictability. James Dean was driving the brand-new Spyder he had purchased from von Neumann in Los Angeles and had brought to Salinas for a sports car race in September 1955 when he suffered his fatal crash. The actor's death made the company name immortal in a market that would contribute handsomely to the transformation of the small house of Porsche into a very big business.

— BRK

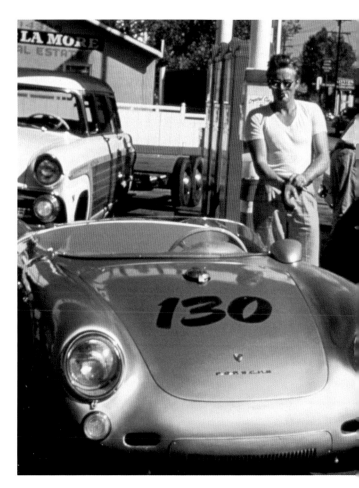

James Dean at a gas station with his silver Porsche 550 Spyder, "Little Bastard," on September 30, 1955, just hours before his fatal crash.

1959 PORSCHE RSK

WINNING RACES is a complicated business. Perpetual redesign is paramount to maintaining a competitive edge. The car on these pages was the ninth and last RSK Spyder built for the factory team and is very different from the first.

The first RSK, 718-001, looked to be a lower version of the Type 550A with the same louvered access doors and lift-off rear body. The Porsches' sports car experience in aerodynamic advantage told them a car five inches closer to the ground would result in a ten-percent reduction in air resistance straightaway. Underneath the RSK, Porsche engineers revised the front suspension and looked for ways to encourage more power. Typically, the car practiced but did not compete upon its first appearance on a race circuit. At the Nürburgring in May 1957, a missed gear shift was the sole malady, which boded well for Le Mans in June where the car appeared dressed in a new wraparound windscreen and quite noticeable squared-off fins to the rear.

Testing had revealed that the redesigned front suspension and new body brought instability. That the tailfin was no cure was dramatically seen during practice at Le Mans when the RSK demonstrated, in the words of reporter Harry Mundy, "the most fantastic spin I have ever seen . . . for fully 350 yards, starting with a slow uncontrolled drift, followed by four slow spins and terminating in four very quick ones." The next day Ferry Porsche and

his son Ferdinand III were at the circuit with a movie camera to record the car at speed, hopefully without any further balletic maneuvers. There was none. But the 718 was no faster down the Mulsanne straight than its predecessor, the 550A, a heavier car by twenty-five pounds. A mid-race collision put the RSK out of Le Mans. It was time to rethink.

Over the winter Porsche engineers discarded the traditional swing-axle/torsion-bar rear suspension for the low-pivot type system Mercedes-Benz was successfully using. More power for the engine necessitated better cooling, which brought more ducting and an oval port in the side of the body, giving the RSK a fresh look. One such car stunned onlookers with its sensational speed at Sebring in 1958 until a gasket in the gearbox gave way. Another placed a splendid second overall in the Targa Florio, proving how vigorous a mere 1½ liters of race car could be.

Nürburgring in 1958 saw two brand-new cars join the square tail-finned RSK, one with a more rounded fin, the other with no fin at all. During practice the former crashed, and drivers of the latter complained of an uncomfortable buoyancy to the rear, so for the race the fins of the car that came to grief were grafted onto the round tail of the finless car, which the

A Porsche RSK (#718) at Nassau, 1958.

drivers declared an improvement. Still, the race did not go well. To fin or not to fin remained an issue. The factory elected not to include any contrivance on the two new cars for Le Mans, one of which placed third overall, which very much impressed the racing world and sent the RSK tailfin to the parts bin of history.

The year 1959 brought a suspension revolution. Swing axles, which in various guise had been part of every Porsche from the first, gave

way to upper and lower wishbones adapted from the type then being used in grand prix racing. From a strategic standpoint, this made sense since a barely disguised raison d'être for the RSK was as a Formula Two exercise to prepare the factory for entry into the grand prix arena of Formula One.

The first outright victory in a manufacturers' championship race followed in the Targa Florio as the new RSK led three other Porsches across the finish line for a clean sweep. The car shown here was used for practice in that event and was sent into battle for the remainder of the season. The most significant race for 718-009 was the Tourist Trophy on the Goodwood Circuit in England on September 5. Porsche lay third in championship points with fifteen against Ferrari's eighteen, and sixteen for Aston Martin. Victory for any of the three would bring the crown.

The drivers of 718-009 were Joakim Bonnier, the twenty-nine-year-old son of a famed geneticist and scion of a powerful publishing family in Stockholm, and Wolfgang Graf Berghe von Trips, who had been born thirty-one years earlier in the family castle near Cologne. The Swedish heir and the German count were superb in their profession and theirs was a brilliant drive. Holding off the 3-liter Aston Martin of Stirling Moss proved an impossible challenge but 718-009 headed Tony Brooks's Ferrari, which also boasted twice the engine capacity of the Porsche, into the final hour of the six-hour race. To do it, 718-009 broke the Class B sports car lap record four times, von Trips doing the final honors at 92.9 mph on the 204th of 205 laps. He finished second, two seconds ahead of Brooks.

Aston Martin took the championship. And Porsche returned to its complicated business. Excellence continued to be expected.

— B R K

A Porsche RSK at Le Mans, 1959.

1965 ASTON MARTIN DB5 VOLANTE

C AN AN INDUSTRIAL concern be considered "romantic"? Aston Martin and its rare DB5 Convertible suggest that it can. More than ninety-five percent of all automotive ventures fail, but this venerable English firm bucked those odds to become one of the world's most famous and revered companies.

Aston's appeal starts with the numerous men who have owned the company since its formation in 1914. Most entrepreneurs enter the business world to make money, others do it because they are passionate about their product. Aston Martin's owners tend to reside in the latter camp, the most prominent of all being Sir David Brown. By 1947, when he purchased the company, the forty-three-year-old Brown had become very wealthy managing a family business that made gears, tractors, and aircraft tugs used by the RAF. He discovered that Aston Martin was for sale almost by accident, from a small classified ad in the London *Times*.

The company's owner at the time was Sir

Arthur Sutherland, a shipping magnate who bought the firm with his son Gordon in 1933. The younger Sutherland skillfully managed it during World War II, avoiding economic catastrophe by manufacturing aircraft components. Aston Martin survived the conflict intact, and was even developing an all-new car, the "Atom." But Sutherland realized he did not have the financial horsepower to see the company through to better times, and he put it on the block. Brown met Sutherland and, as a keen driver during his teens and twenties, gleefully took the Atom out for a thorough test drive. The industrialist felt the one-off prototype would be "fun to have and play around with," so he bought the company "more or less on a whim." The cost was £20,000.

Shortly after the ownership change was announced, in February 1947, Brown acquired another company to obtain the right engine to power his cars. Lagonda had been formed in 1906, named after a creek running through Springfield, Ohio. Its founder was an American-born opera singer who became a motorcycle manufacturer when his dream of operatic fame fizzled. Lagonda's advanced 2.5-liter engine, designed by W. O. Bentley, was, in Brown's words, "already built, tried, and tested." The firm would eventually cost him more than double the price of Aston Martin. Yet Brown couldn't have been happier. He owned Aston Martin Lagonda Ltd. for the better part of three decades, reportedly losing money on nearly every car he made.

Such passion is part of the Aston mystique, but the company is also romantic for its

underdog—and ultimately triumphant—role in international competition. Its racing history is filled with stories of luck, whimsy, and awfully long odds. Starting in 1948 Brown and his men embarked on an eleven-year odyssey to win the race at Le Mans and the world endurance championship. On the suggestion of a newly hired employee, the company entered a race at Spa and, after a frantic nine weeks of building the DB1 (for "David Brown, first model") in the fall of 1948, they won it.

The DB2, unveiled the following year, was a true dual-purpose car. A handsome and capable performer, the DB2 placed consistently in the top five at many of the world's great races during its first few years of production, its most notable finish a third overall at Le Mans in 1951. It sold well as a street car and soldiered on into the late 1950s in various guises. One of them would star in Alfred Hitchcock's classic thriller *The Birds*.

But early on in the process, Aston recognized it needed purpose-built cars if it truly wished to compete for the crown. Throughout the decade, the company fielded models such as the DB3 and DB3S to battle more experienced and often better-funded competitors like Mercedes, Jaguar, Porsche, and Ferrari, but it wasn't until 1959 that it finally prevailed.

The chariot of choice was the DBR1, a beautiful, well-balanced race car that was powered by a lusty 6-cylinder engine. That year everything came together—a victory at Le Mans and the capturing of the championship, edging out Ferrari in a closely contested battle. Having made its point, Aston then retired from competing full-time.

Lessons learned in competition make an Aston Martin one of the most exhilarating of traveling companions. An Aston at speed is an ethereal experience. Its road agility remains otherworldly—like hitting the dance floor in your favorite pair of shoes. Its immense power is obvious, yet it is all beautifully controllable. Such sensations were especially coveted after the war, and were rarely found in any motorcar. In the forties, fifties, and sixties, long-distance travel was more of an adventure, and one hundred miles an hour an incredible speed. Widespread airplane travel was still off in the future, so the wealthy used their *gran turismos* frequently. Wherever they went, Astons were admired as more than "just" hand-built cars capable of getting their occupants from A to B in comfort. They were mobile fashion statements that represented the best England and the automotive world had to offer.

One of the most delectable of all was the DB5

Convertible. Its formal name was the DB5 Drop Head Coupe, and just over 120 were made between 1963 and 1965. Its covered headlights, long hood, and sexy fenders made it look sensational whether the top was up or down. The car's body fit neatly over its robust chassis like a slinky black dress on a fashion model, causing anyone who saw it to stare. And why not? In many ways, the DB5 Convertible, like all of Aston's offerings, was tailored to fit its owner. When desired, materials and colors were made to specification.

Then, just as DB5 Convertible production was winding down, Aston Martin vaulted beyond the cognoscenti's radar screen to become a household word. Its coupe sibling became an international star when a certain Agent 007 made it the most famous car in the world. Young boys everywhere (and many of their fathers) were soon wondering why the family car didn't look so cool and sound so good, and why it didn't have ejector seats and machine guns behind the lights. Corgi Toys quickly had a bestseller on its hands with a scale-model version, and the *Goldfinger* DB5 went on tour around the globe, capped by a starring role at the 1965 World's Fair in New York.

The DB5 remained a high point for Aston Martin for quite some time. Brown owned the

James Bond in Paris: an Aston Martin DB5 at the French premiere of *Goldfinger*.

company until 1972, when he sold it for one hundred pounds sterling and the assumption of debt. Aston Martin then went through another string of owners until Ford Motor Company acquired it in the late 1980s. In recognition of Sir David Brown's legacy (he was knighted in 1968), Aston returned to using the "DB" model designation after more than a twenty-year gap with the new DB7, which debuted in 1993.

Brown was thrilled by the touch. He passed away shortly after the model's introduction, honored to see his legacy come full circle.
— wsg

1960 FERRARI 250 GT SWB BERLINETTA SCAGLIETTI

I F ONE SHAPE came to represent Italian style after World War II, it was the *berlinetta*, Italian for "little sedan." The word is commonly used to describe the design most Americans would call a "fastback." One of the most artistic and pleasing automotive shapes, the classic Italian *berlinetta* was (and is) almost always a two-seater that features a flowing hood and sloping rear roofline. The design's silhouette is simplicity, its proportions nothing short of superb. The form is tasteful and elegant and can create tension through rounded surfaces such as the shoulders over the rear wheels.

The postwar master of the *berlinetta* has been Industrie Pininfarina S.p.A., and company founder Battista Pininfarina began experimenting with the shape in the 1930s. "My father was instinctively an aerodynamicist," said Sergio Pininfarina. "He believed aerodynamics were very, very important for speed, performance, and safety," whereas most automobile makers "were more fond of the power of the engine." That had become clear to the

world in 1936, when Pininfarina created the experimental Lancia Aprilia, a small sedan for the masses. For much of that decade he observed how the wind influenced shapes in nature, particularly its effects on snow. Pininfarina had his men replace the standard body with a smooth nose and long tapering tail that resembled an airplane wing. The idea behind

Pininfarina and his son Sergio examining the engine of the new Alfa Romeo, 1956.

the design is what Pinin called "essentiality." As he later observed, "What you take off counts more than what you add on." Changing the body saw the car's top speed improve from 75 mph to almost 100. Pininfarina was now convinced of the importance of a car's aerodynamics, and the fastback's role in achieving them.

After World War II, Pinin worked with the Turin-based industrialist Piero Dusio and his company Cisitalia, creating a landmark *berlinetta* design for its 202 model. First seen in 1947, the Cisitalia 202 would influence the Ferrari 250 SWB and just about every other enclosed sports car. Its clean, uncluttered form exhibited stupendous balance, and it was the first car with a front-mounted engine that had a hood lower than the fenders. Its impact was so great that *Road & Track* ran two separate columns begging a domestic manufacturer to obtain the rights to the design. In 1951 a Cisitalia 202 was placed on permanent exhibit in New York's Museum of Modern Art, the star of the museum's groundbreaking exhibition, "Eight Automobiles." "The Cisitalia's body is

slipped over its chassis like a dust jacket over a book," was how the show's catalogue beautifully summed up Pininfarina's masterwork.

Once the Ferrari-Pininfarina relationship began in 1952, the coachbuilder started creating breathtaking designs that found their roots in 1947's Cisitalia. The 250 and 375 MM models of 1953 to 1955 also had superb proportioning, long hoods, and flowing fastbacks in the continual pursuit of aerodynamic efficiency. The 250 GT Competizione and "Tour de France" —the latter named after the car's dominance of the grueling French race in the later 1950s —were a further evolution of the theme.

But the high point of the Ferrari *berlinetta* from the 1950s was the 250 SWB. Called by Sergio Pininfarina "the first of our three quantum leaps in designs on Ferrari," the "SWB" stands for short wheelbase, referring to the shorter distance between the front and rear wheels when compared to its immediate predecessors. The 250, as was standard Ferrari practice, represented the cubic capacity of one of the 3-liter V12's cylinders.

The 250 SWB was one of history's ultimate "dual-purpose" road cars—machines that are equally at home on the street or racetrack. When this Ferrari was built in the late 1950s to early 1960s, one could order it with a steel body and comfortable leather interior, or in lightweight aluminum with bare interior and higher horsepower motor—the perfect combination to win a class at races such as Le Mans and Sebring.

The fact that the 250 SWB looks so right on either kind of road can be traced back to the eye of Battista Pininfarina and the company's design and construction techniques. Tom Tjaarda, a noted American designer who worked at Pininfarina during the last two years of SWB production, said, "Cars like the Ferrari 250 SWB not only displayed beautiful shapes but also sensitive surface development and proportions which, even today, still look right. This was Italian design and it came from their cultural heritage, because the men who designed cars were never trained in styling. They were endowed with a natural instinct and taste for what was right in the delicate balance between line and mass. This artistic culture dates back to classic Greek architecture, when line and curves were adjusted for the eye to view them from any angle."

What made Pinin able to create such seminal shapes without any training was an eye that went beyond extraordinary. Tjaarda found this out as he worked on a one-off Pininfarina show car the year after 250 SWB production ended. He recalls the great designer looking at a full-scale plaster mock-up, then telling his men to take five millimeters off it to make the car's appearance tauter. But rather than do as instructed, the group decided simply to paint the model, knowing it would appear smaller when seen in a color other than white. When Pinin viewed the model a few days later, he first nodded in approval, and then said, "I hate to tell you this, but the design still isn't right. We'll need to take off another five millimeters." That type of exacting eye is what made the 250 SWB such an influential masterpiece.

—WSG

1960 FERRARI 250 GT SPYDER CALIFORNIA

AS GIFTED AS Pininfarina was at making flowing fastback designs, he and his men were equally adept at creating two-seat roadsters, or "spyders," as the Italians call them, often spelled with a *y* to retain the English pronunciation. The 250 GT Spyder California is one of the best —sleek, sensual, and with exhilarating road manners. Approximately one hundred were made between 1958 and 1963.

According to former Ferrari sales manager Girolamo Gardini, the 250 GT Spyder California was the brainchild of Ferrari's California importer Johnny von Neumann, one of Ferrari's largest clients in the 1950s, who asked the company for "a simple spyder." He would get that, and more. The resulting masterpiece in metal resembles certain types of fashion or artistic trends in that its shape so perfectly represents the social and economic climate found during the era in which it was created. This Ferrari's effervescent personality can be attributed to several factors: what the state of California represented at the time, the arti-

sans who made the car, Ferrari's desire to race, and a positive business and social climate the Italians called the "economic miracle."

It took the country several years to put the devastation of World War II behind it—both physically and psychologically. By the early 1950s, with the privations of the postwar years in the past, Europeans were once again becoming comfortable spending money and flaunting their affluence and success. Their optimism about the future was reflected in the way they lived. Construction was occurring everywhere one looked, and work was a valuable commodity cherished by entrepreneurs and workers alike. Incomes rose annually, and everyone expected the next year to be better than the last. Fun and glamour became "in" things, and Italy seemed to grasp the two concepts better than any other country.

Among the great beneficiaries of that prosperous time were Italy's *capitani d'industrie*, who operated in an environment virtually free of restraints and "practically established Italy's postwar style," says Piero Rivolta, the son of

one of Milan's noted *capitani*. For this industrial ruling class, one of the most cherished
possessions was a fast sports *gran turismo*, or
GT. Not only were these cars a tasteful way to
show off one's wealth and success, but they
could be used as a rapid means of transport—
in an era when commuter flights were hardly
the norm—to visit factories across Italy and
Europe.

That made racing all the more imperative
for builders like Enzo Ferrari. Competition
was the ultimate demonstration of mechanical reliability in a period when long-distance
car travel was still an adventure. Races were
the ideal advertising medium because the general populace widely followed them. And indeed, demand for cars such as Ferraris boomed
throughout the decade. According to the Ferrari factory records, in 1950 the firm produced
twenty-six cars. Ten years later production had
increased more than 1,000 percent to over
three hundred, and that type of expansion was
not limited to sports car manufacture. New
customers were appearing every year in droves,

making *gran turismo* production a growth
industry.

Sergio Pininfarina was well aware of this
expansion and, as with his client Ferrari, his
construction methods underwent a transformation in the 1950s. Cars were still made by
hand but no longer were they crafted like
individual suits where each was completely
different. Customers wanted refinement, and
the only way to guarantee that was with more
sophisticated development and manufacturing techniques, and larger production runs.

Throughout the 1950s, as the company expanded, Pininfarina's craftsmen and stylists
often worked "on the razor's edge," in the
words of designer Franco Martinengo. This led
to the continual experimentation and refinement of design themes. A wooden body buck
would be modified slightly, or the men might
take the buck or resulting metal form for a certain body piece or design element and use it
on another car.

Look no further than the two earliest Pininfarina spyders in this book (pages 98 and

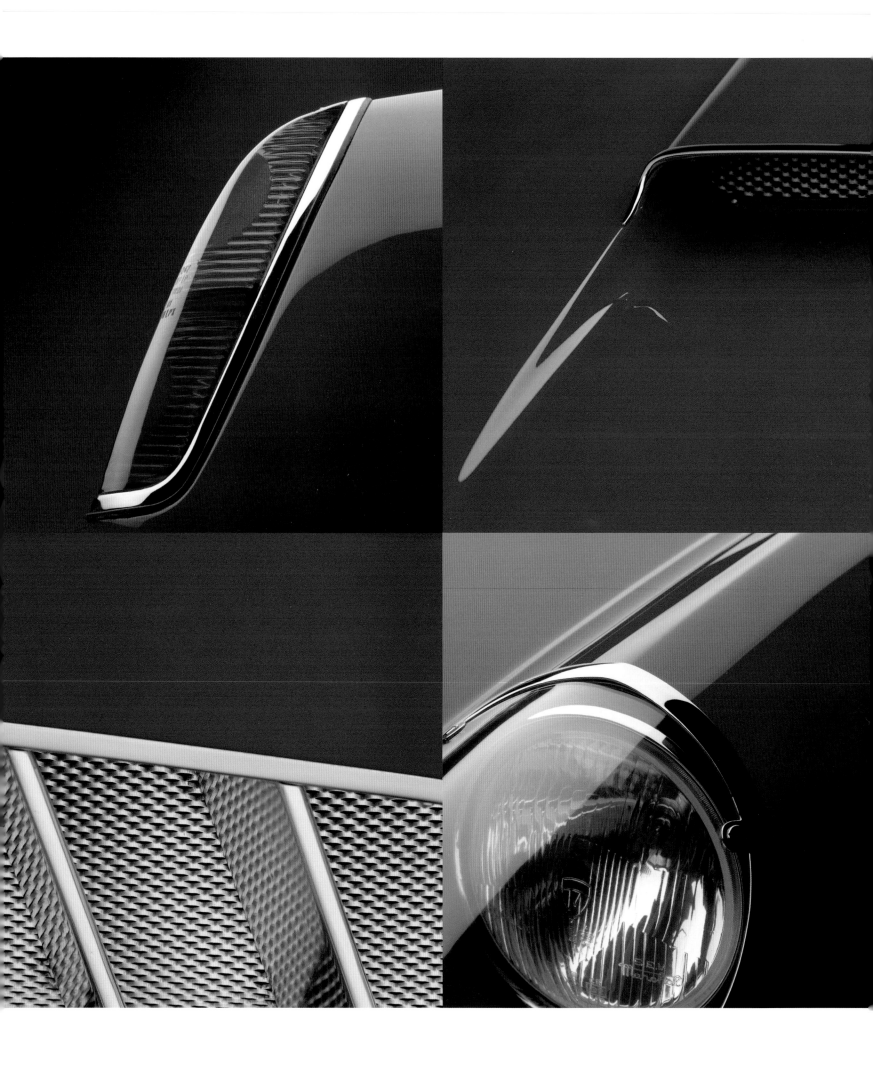

A Spyder California piloted by Jo Schlesser about to enter the Mulsanne Straight at Le Mans, 1960.

The 250 cabriolet looks remarkably similar to the 250 Spyder California, making it seem that the California is a Pininfarina creation. But it is not so simple, for unlike the cabriolet, Ferrari had Scaglietti make the California's body. The Spyder California was, in fact, one of the earliest joint collaborations between two legendary coachbuilders. Sergio Pininfarina recalled their differences in personal style: "[Scaglietti] was a man with no tradition or culture. When you looked at the shoes, the way he spoke, he was very much a countryman. On the contrary, I was young, refined and educated, like a young lord." Despite this, "Scaglietti was very kind to me and we worked very well together." Indeed, the process was so collaborative that neither man has taken credit for its world-renowned shape. When Scaglietti was asked who designed it, he said it was Pininfarina. When the same question was posed to Pininfarina, he credited Scaglietti.

Regardless, the end result is a piece of art that was equally at home on southern California's Sunset Boulevard, the Amalfi coast, or running flat out on the Mulsanne Straight during Le Mans. One placed fifth overall at the famed French endurance race in 1959, while another three finished in the top ten at Sebring the following year.

This particular Spyder California, chassis 2167 GT, demonstrates the car's "dual purpose" nature. Ferrari historian Marcel Massini's records show that it was constructed several months after the 1960 Sebring race, where the model dotted the top ten placings. It competed in 1961, finishing first in class in a hill climb race in June. It also raced the following year, then was used exclusively as a street car.

Looking at this seminal Ferrari today, the design remains as alluring and as pure as ever. It beckons you to run your hands across its superb surfaces, fire up the engine, and get a sense of what the good life was all about more than four decades ago.

—WSG

113) to see the two-seat open-air theme evolve. The breathtaking front-to-rear proportioning on the 375 Plus still exists on the 250 Spyder California. Pininfarina first used recessed covered headlights in 1954 to aid aerodynamics, and they are found on the 250. The lovely haunch over the rear wheel, a masterstroke that gives Pininfarina's designs power and sensual lines, is on both cars. The spyder theme became smaller, lighter, and sleeker as it progressed, achieving a high point in 1957 when Pininfarina created a magnificent series of 250 GT cabriolets. Each was hand built and had the same general lines, but details differed between cars. One had a cut-down section in the driver's door, another a headrest behind the driver's seat, much like the 1958 Testa Rossa (see pages 107–111). After the first handful, production became more standardized, with only such details as colors, vents, and bumpers varying from car to car.

1964 FERRARI 250LM

THERE ARE TWO basic schools of thought in car design: styling and functionalism — the pursuit of beauty or the pursuit of efficiency. Mid-engine cars are a perfect example of functionalism. By placing the engine behind the driver, the designer doesn't have to worry about restrictions caused by the engine's height and size, leaving much greater freedom to make the front of the car as aerodynamic as possible. Further, having the engine's mass in the center of the chassis promotes better cornering. The physics of a front-engine car is like that of a pendulum swinging. A mid-engine design eliminates this, allowing the engineers to make the car lower to the ground because they don't have to worry about under-chassis components such as the exhaust system.

Enzo Ferrari's machines were typically conservative in their engineering design, their winning edge brought about by refining long-proven techniques and superior mechanical reliability. Still, having a proven design didn't stop Ferrari's engineering staff from losing sleep in the late 1950s, and among those tossing and turning was Carlo Chiti.

A large, gregarious character and the company's technical director, Chiti was then in his early thirties, having cut his teeth in Alfa's engineering department through much of the 1950s. In 1957 fellow engineer Giotto Bizzarrini lured him to Ferrari. During Chiti's first full year at Ferrari, Ferrari driver Mike Hawthorne won the driver's championship, and the Ferrari team placed second in the constructor's championship. But that didn't stop Chiti from being restless. He had a clear vision of where the future lay, and all one had to do was look at the English builders to see it.

Chiti's realization began in early January 1958, when Ferrari traveled to Argentina for the grand prix, expecting to win the race. Much to their surprise, they came in second to Stirling Moss in a Cooper-Climax with considerably less power. Four months later Ferrari finished in the same position at Monaco, losing to another mid-engine Cooper. In Argentina Chiti had attributed the Cooper's prowess to Moss's legendary driving skills. But Maurice Trintignant's win at Monaco showed that more than driving talent lay behind the car's success.

During the 1959 season, Chiti started campaigning to revolutionize Ferrari's race cars. It was an uphill battle, for Ferrari believed that a Formula One car with a rear engine would be a betrayal of the company's technical philosophy. But when Ferrari lost the championship that year to Cooper in Formula One and Aston Martin in endurance racing, other voices began chiming in, and the "Old Man" finally relented.

The mid/rear-engine formula was first tried in 1960 on two single-seat cars—one for Formula One, the other for Formula Two. Ferrari's first mid-engine endurance racer, the 246 SP, came a few months later. Underneath its rakish spyder coachwork by Fantuzzi was a slightly modified version of the Formula One chassis with two seats. The 246 SP competed in several races during the 1961 campaign, scoring a victory and third-place finish.

A great influence on race car design is racing regulations, and after the 1963 season the rules stated that prototypes could once again use 3-liter engines. This worked in Ferrari's favor, for its 250 engine had evolved considerably over the past several years and would win another championship for the company in 1962 with the 250 GTO.

Mauro Forghieri, who had taken over for Chiti after the Ferrari "walkout" in 1961, im-

mediately recognized the potential to combine the 250 engine with a modified Dino chassis, and so was born the 250P. The P stood for *prototipo*, while the 250, in typical Ferrari fashion, was the size in cubic centimeters of one engine cylinder. The racing Dino chassis was lengthened to accommodate the larger engine, and a lovely two-seat body that featured an open, targa-style (partially removable) roof was draped over the mechanicals. The 250P was a stellar performer. During the 1963 season, it competed in the prototype class and won three of the championship's four most important races, including Le Mans. Now convinced that the future for competition cars lay in mid-engine designs, Enzo Ferrari decided to create a new mid-engine GT for the championship class. The 250P was an obvious starting point, so Pininfarina took the basic design and turned it into a closed coupe, the 250LM.

The LM stood for "Le Mans," and the prototype was first shown at the Paris Auto Show in October 1963 to great fanfare. In the LM, Pininfarina presented a great case study in how form following function can still be beautiful. The car's nose is graceful and efficient, everything created to cleanly cut the air and push the front downward for superior handling. Scoops funnel air to the brakes, and the wind-

shield has a steep rake that is both lovely and essential. The rear is a study in the sensuality of efficiency. The bulging rear fenders have a voluptuous curve, with intake at the front to funnel air to the engine. The back of the cabin's rearward taper is fluid in its form, flowing into the rounded shoulders over the rear wheels. A small spoiler is integrated into the tail and has a soft upward sweep to finish off the design in sensational fashion.

Only the prototype 250LM would use the 3-liter V12, for all subsequent LMs had a more powerful 3.3-liter V12. Ferrari, however, never changed the name to 275LM, though this would have been more accurate. In order to qualify for championship class, as opposed to the more grueling prototype class, the rules of the Fédération Internationale de l'Automobile (FIA) stated that at least one hundred of a particular model had to be built. By retaining the name 250LM, Ferrari hoped to include production numbers from the earlier model and have his new car qualify for competition class. But the FIA was not fooled, and it ruled that the LM was too different from any of its predecessors. The new 250LM would have to run in prototype class against faster, more powerful competition that included some of Ferrari's own racing models.

The FIA's decision was prescient, for only thirty-two LMs would be made between 1963 and 1965. But that did not stop it from becoming an integral part of the Ferrari legend. In 1964, out of the thirty-five races in which LMs participated, they won ten. The following year a 250LM from American importer Luigi Chinetti's North American Racing Team (NART) won the biggest prize of all—overall victory at Le Mans.

—WSG

1965 FERRARI 275 P2/3 SPYDER DROGO

HE 275 P2/3 was a combatant in a true David vs. Goliath scenario that highlights the mystique surrounding the Modena area. The Goliath was America's Ford Motor Company. Founded in 1903, the firm was the world's second largest auto manufacturer by the time the 275 P2/3 was born in the mid-1960s. In the U.S. alone, Ford employed more than 175,000 people and produced an average of 6,562 cars per day. On top of that, the company had manufacturing and assembly plants in almost twenty other countries. As one Ford executive recently chuckled about the company's finances, "We lost more in rounding our figures than Ferrari made in a year."

Ferrari's production, meanwhile, hovered around seven hundred cars, and would not reach the one-thousand mark until 1971. At the center of it all was Enzo Ferrari, often described as "an agitator of men." That the company employed only five hundred people belied its stature in the world. The endurance racing championship was first run in 1953 and, up to 1966, when the P2/3 was made, Ferrari had won it eleven times. No other company had even won two championships. The results were much the same in Formula One racing, which Ferrari had won six times—triple the record of its closest competitors.

That luster appealed to the Ford Motor Company in the early 1960s. The American concern was then starting to target a more youthful audience. Performance was the hot ticket, and nothing shouted performance better than competition on the racetrack. When one spoke about continued success in competition, the list started and ended with Ferrari.

Ferrari entered Ford's radar screen in January 1963, when chairman Henry Ford II and Lee Iacocca, then a rising star in the company, came up with the idea of purchasing Ferrari to jump-start Ford's assault on the burgeoning performance-oriented marketplace. Ferrari was in fact for sale at the time, and was being wooed by the Mecom family from Texas, though when the Mecoms learned of Ford's interest they backed away. Ford's first contact with Ferrari was made in May 1963 through Ford's Italian subsidiary. The framework for a deal was settled upon fairly quickly, the new structure calling for two companies: Ford-Ferrari to make the street *gran turismos* that Ferrari was already building, and Ferrari-Ford to construct the competition cars. Ford would be the majority shareholder of the former, Enzo Ferrari the largest shareholder of the latter. Negotiations collapsed after ten days, however, when it became clear that Ferrari wanted to maintain complete control of Ferrari-Ford. Donald Frey, who had spearheaded the talks for Ford, returned home to report to Henry Ford II. Ford's response after the briefing was simply, "That's okay. Let's go beat them."

The ensuing battle lasted the better part of five years. Ford's weapon was the GT40, a beautiful mid-engine race car developed with all the resources of the Ford organization behind it. But economic might doesn't guarantee right. In 1964, GT40s powered by 4.7-liter V8 engines performed less well than expected, so Ford responded in a proper American hot-rod

way—make the engine bigger. That led to the creation of the 7-liter GT40 Mk II, which first appeared at Le Mans in 1965.

Ferrari, meanwhile, was not idle after the deal with Ford fell apart. He, too, recognized that "there is no substitute for cubic inches," and so were born the 275P and 330P in 1964. These two machines had more powerful engines than the 250LM and bodies that were longer, wider, and sleeker. They would place first at events such as Le Mans and Sebring.

The following year Ferrari again responded to the Ford challenge with the 275P2, 330P2, 365P2, and 365P. The new models had a more purposeful air than 1964's 275P, and the cars' handcrafted aluminum skin hid a number of mechanical updates. The chassis used Formula One-derived construction techniques to make them lighter and stronger. The suspension was improved and the engine massaged for even greater power. The V12s now had two spark plugs per cylinder, which boosted horsepower much the way two candles light a room better than one. The modifications were successful, to say the least. P2s would win at events such as Sicily's grueling Targa Florio and power

Ferrari to the Prototype Trophy, trouncing the third-place Ford 79.8 to 19.6 points (second place went to Porsche). Still, thanks to the efforts of racing champion and car builder Carroll Shelby, Ford won the more important GT Manufacturer's Championship.

The P2 shown here, chassis 0826, was in the thick of the battle in 1965. It showed at Le Mans and would run as high as third place but would not finish the race because of mechanical problems. Two weeks later it competed again in Reims, where it placed second while setting a lap record. The car remained a part of the company's racing arsenal the following year, and would be substantially modified into its current configuration. To offset the Ford onslaught, the power of Ferrari's race cars was upped once again, the chassis was up-dated, and the bodies became even more aerodynamic.

Piero Drogo, the person widely credited with creating 0826's coachwork, is something of a mystery man in the history of auto racing. He worked for the evocatively named Carrozzeria Sports Cars, one of many coachbuilders dotting the Modena landscape, hoping to become the next Scaglietti. But Drogo took a far differ-

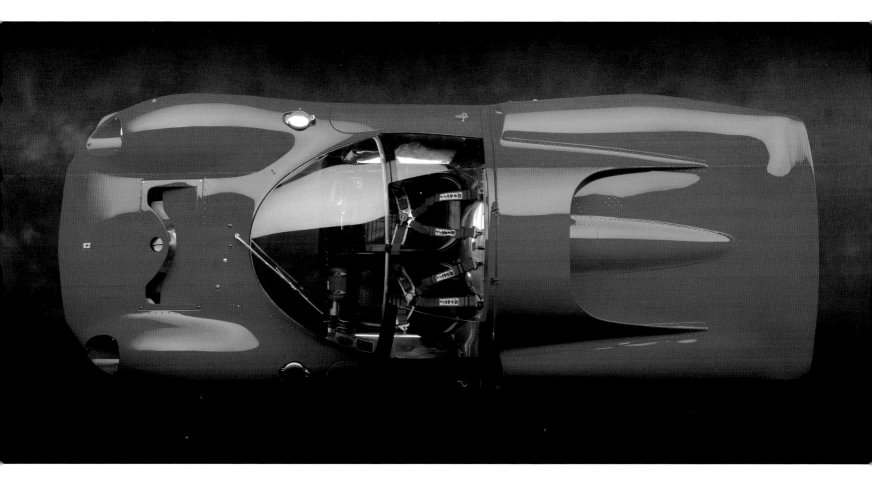

ent path from his world-famous role model. It has long been written that Drogo hailed from Argentina and emigrated to the Modena area, but research by historian Adolfo Orsi shows that Drogo actually came from Alessandria, a city on the southern outskirts of Turin some 150 miles north of Modena.

Very little is known about Drogo's early years. He first appeared on the Modena scene in the mid- to late 1950s, not as a coachbuilder but as a racing driver, and might have spent some time working for Maserati. In the early 1960s Drogo started making a name for himself with Carrozzeria Sports Cars. One early client was Count Giovanni Volpi and his Scuderia Serenissima, for which Sports Cars made race car bodies such as the "Breadvan." Drogo also made a number of bodies for engineer Giotto Bizzarrini in 1964 and 1965.

Though Drogo's name is associated with coachwork, he was not a panelbeater or stylist. Instead he was the Carrozzeria Sports Cars's front man, working closely with the firm's shareholders and its commercial clients. Nor did he particularly enjoy Ferrari's favor; rather he happened to be in the right place at the right time when Ferrari needed work done and others such as Scaglietti were completely booked.

The new coachwork Drogo's men created for chassis 0826 was purposeful and voluptuous. Everything was changed from its earlier configuration to make it more efficient at penetrating the air and cooling components. But 0826's competition career in its new guise would be brief, the Ferrari lasting just two hours at Le Mans in 1966 before it was sidelined with mechanical failure. It then retired from racing.

Ford went on to win Le Mans and the world championship that year. But the underdog returned with a vengeance in 1967, when Ferrari snared another world championship with an even faster 330P4. That victory would be Ferrari's twelfth endurance crown. Like the eleven preceding it, the 1967 championship also acted as a carrot, enticing numerous "unknowns" to Modena. All would arrive hoping to make names for themselves, just as Piero Drogo had done in the 1950s and '60s.

—wsg

1967 FERRARI 275 GTB/4 NART SPYDER

FERRARI WAS on a roll when the 275 NART Spyder was born. The company's production had expanded greatly during the 1960s, jumping from approximately three hundred at the beginning of the decade to over seven hundred by 1967. Ferrari would win another endurance championship that year, the sixth in eight years.

The range of models the company offered also had never been greater. The new V6-powered 206 Dino was the result of Sergio Pininfarina's relentless push for a mid-engine Ferrari. The 330 GTC was available for those who wanted refinement and understated elegance, and the GTS version appealed to clients desiring comfort with wind-in-the-hair exhilaration. The 365 California was the last of the custom coachwork Ferraris that could be ordered through a dealership, and the 330 2+2 was a fast touring car for four.

In 1967 the sexiest, highest performing street Ferrari was the 275 GTB/4. Introduced in 1964 as the 275 GTB (for *gran turismo berlinetta*), this classic fastback defined the word "exotic" from the mid-1960s, with its long nose, voluptuous front and rear fenders, and taut cabin. The 275 GTB/4, introduced in 1966, was Ferrari's response to the jet set's increasing demand for speed. At the time in Italy, home to the world's fastest, most prestigious car manufacturers, what you owned and how quickly it would go was a big topic of discussion at swank cocktail parties. As one *gran turismo* constructor would recall, whether someone went from Milan to Turin in 31 or 32 minutes suddenly became very important.

Ferrari had long enjoyed a reputation as maker of the fastest cars, but that title was now under serious assault. Maserati's new Ghibli had a top speed listed at over 170 mph, as did Lamborghini's mid-engine Miura, while newcomer Iso's two-seat Grifo cleared 160 mph in numerous magazine tests. The 275 GTB/4 put more power under that long hood, bumping horsepower up to 300 from the standard 275 GTB's 260. Top speed was listed in excess of 160 mph.

Pininfarina may have designed the car but

the man making the bodies was Ferrari's old friend Sergio Scaglietti. Scaglietti hardly noticed the economic boom occurring around Modena. And while his and Ferrari's firms continued to get bigger, he was most appreciative that the "Old Man" didn't change his ways. Their friendship and business relationship remained as close as ever. Which is why, when Luigi Chinetti approached Scaglietti about making a special open-air version of the 275 GTB/4 for the American market, it was destined to happen. Chinetti is another major name in Ferrari history, the man who brought Ferrari to America.

Ferrari could not have had a better representative than Chinetti, who was both a successful importer and an admirable racing driver in his own right. In 1948 he sold the very first 166 *barchetta* off the stand at the Turin Auto Show, and the following year drove *barchettas* to win both Le Mans and the twenty-four hours of Spa. Such exploits brought great publicity to Ferrari in North America, boosting Chinetti's and Ferrari's fortunes.

In 1956 Chinetti formed the North American Racing Team with backing from wealthy racers George Arents and Jan de Vroom. Chinetti's close relationship with Ferrari ensured he obtained a consistent string of competitive cars. NART also acted as a springboard for a number of top drivers, such as world champions Mario Andretti and Phil Hill. Through the 1960s NART competed at the world's top races, often winning at such venues as Daytona. Then, in 1965, a NART-entered 250LM became the last Ferrari to win Le Mans.

After the 275 GTB/4 was introduced in 1966, Chinetti approached Enzo Ferrari about making an open-air version of the car. The idea was struck down, but Chinetti knew his way around the Ferrari circles and spoke with Scaglietti. An agreement was soon struck, and Scaglietti went to work making Chinetti the ten cars he ordered.

The NART Spyder quickly became one of the outstanding cars on the market. One placed seventeenth overall at Sebring in 1967, while another would star in the original *Thomas Crown*

Affair with Steve McQueen and Faye Dunaway. *Road & Track*'s September 1967 issue featured the Sebring car on the cover, dubbing it "the most satisfying sports car in the world."

Such accolades and high profile make it surprising to learn that Chinetti struggled to sell the ten he had in stock. As he later admitted, not one brought list price, and he ended up getting rid of the last few by discounting the cost to below that of the standard 275 GTB/4 coupe. Today NART Spyders are one of the most valuable street Ferraris, normally sold in private transactions like art objects.

With hindsight, it becomes clear that the NART Spyder marked a turning point in Ferrari history. It would be the last Ferrari model that a patron such as Chinetti could specially order. And in 1968 America's new emissions and safety standards caused small manufacturers such as Ferrari to focus on meeting the new requirements, rather than designing, engineering, and building limited-run models. Meanwhile, changes in the social climate in Italy and Europe had Ferrari and Scaglietti constantly battling the unions. That development in particular caused Ferrari to sell half his company to Fiat in 1969, including the Scaglietti works. Sergio Scaglietti would manage the *carrozzeria* that bore his name for the next sixteen years, then retire in 1986. Today he smiles on the good fortune and fame life brought him, all thanks to his relationship with Enzo Ferrari.

— W S G

1973 FERRARI 365 GTB/4 DAYTONA SPYDER

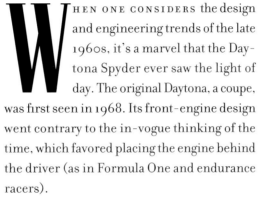

WHEN ONE CONSIDERS the design and engineering trends of the late 1960s, it's a marvel that the Daytona Spyder ever saw the light of day. The original Daytona, a coupe, was first seen in 1968. Its front-engine design went contrary to the in-vogue thinking of the time, which favored placing the engine behind the driver (as in Formula One and endurance racers).

Sergio Pininfarina was all too aware of the mid-engine revolution in its earliest days. At the 1965 Turin Auto Show, an intriguing naked chassis was on display, its V12 engine mounted sideways behind the passenger compartment. Unfortunately, the chassis was not on Ferrari's stand, but that of a troubling newcomer, Lamborghini. "When I saw that chassis," he recalls, "I was envious."

He had every reason to be. The mid-engine configuration offered the ultimate in high-performance design, giving a stylist more freedom, particularly in aerodynamics. Over the prior several months Pininfarina had tried to convince Ferrari to produce a mid-engine street car, but Ferrari dug in his heels. He felt that a mid-engine design was fine for racing but too dangerous for customers, and he did not want his race cars to be designed differently from his road cars. Pininfarina's envy only increased when Lamborghini's prototype Miura debuted four months later at Geneva, changing the performance-car equation in the process. Yet, even its startling shape and the unprecedented market and press reaction it garnered wasn't enough to persuade the "Old Man."

At that point, Pininfarina stylist Leonardo Fioravanti stumbled across a chassis in the Pininfarina works belonging to Ferrari's newest model, the 330 GTC/GTS. Inspired by what he saw, he put pen to paper in an effort to design the ideal body for the chassis. Of key importance were the car's general proportions—he wanted to faithfully follow the overall dimensions of the mechanical parts while paying extreme attention to aerodynamics.

Despite his ongoing debate with Ferrari over a mid-engine car, Pininfarina recognized a great design when he saw one, and he instructed Fioravanti to make some formal renderings to present to Ferrari. As Pininfarina recalled, the design's fundamental objective was to "obtain a thin, svelte car like a mid-engine design." The challenge was that the forward engine meant having to run the exhaust system under the car, which made it look taller. The design thus became a search for a sense of lightness and rake.

As was customary, after the renderings were completed and sent to Ferrari, in December 1966, they were made into wooden or resin models, which Ferrari would travel to Turin to examine. These meetings often resulted in spirited exchanges as technical alterations were deliberated, and designing the Daytona would be no different. After Ferrari made his choice on styling renderings, Fioravanti began work on the "form plan," a type of blueprint drawing that served as a starting point for the construction of the full-scale model prototype. The form plan was completed in January 1967 and given the green light. Construction was to be handled by Sergio Scaglietti.

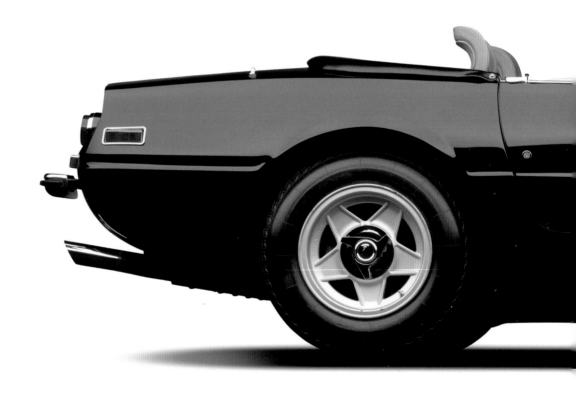

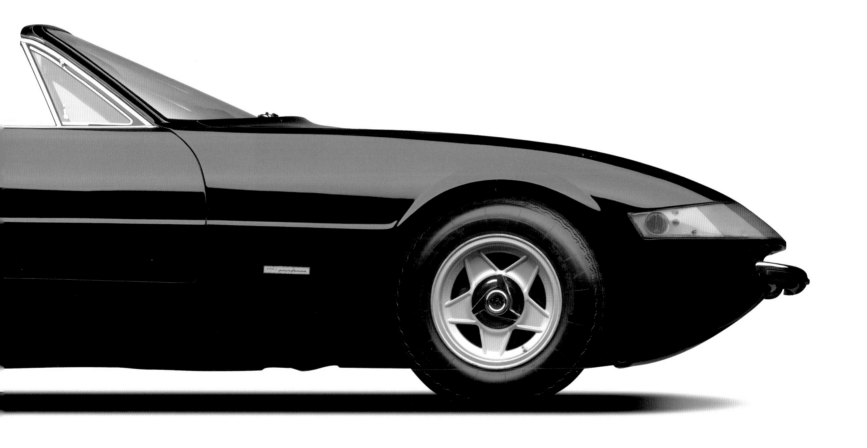

That Scaglietti was involved in the Daytona story was natural, given his history of building Ferrari's race car bodies since the early 1950s and the vast majority of street car bodies in the 1960s. And though his role as a designer was basically over by this time, styling still boiled in Sergio's blood. The coachbuilder often put his own touch on Pininfarina's designs.

What makes the Daytona's construction memorable for Scaglietti was Enzo's reaction: It was the only time he saw his famous friend lose his temper—twice. The first time was in the Scaglietti works, when Ferrari shouted that he didn't like the job at all. His reaction caused Scaglietti to change the front to something more typical of his style. Then Ferrari's technical team became involved and felt the car's width was too narrow. After another tirade, Scaglietti and his men cut the model down the middle to add a few more centimeters. Finally, in mid-1968, Ferrari signed off on its appearance.

The Daytona was first shown at the 1968 Paris Auto Show. Called "365 GTB/4" by the factory, the "Daytona" moniker referred to Ferrari's one-two-three sweep at the famed Florida racetrack the previous year. Underneath the long hood was an all-new 352-horsepower V12 engine that gave the model a top speed of 174 mph.

That the engine was still up front did not matter to the critics, for the world soon learned that the "anti-Miura," as England's *Motor* dubbed the Daytona in reference to Lamborghini's mid-engine road car, was *the* performance machine to have. "It might as well be said right now," began *Road & Track*'s October 1970 test that echoed the sentiments of every other magazine's test, "The Ferrari 365 GTB/4 is the best sports car in the world. Or the best GT. Take your choice: it's both. And we really didn't expect it to be. After all, it's not the most exotic—the engine is still up front."

Despite its success, Fioravanti never

planned to have a spyder model when he originally sketched the Daytona coupe. He simply envisaged a very high performance car, one in which structural rigidity and aerodynamic considerations were of paramount importance. A car without a roof greatly compromises those two goals. That, however, didn't deter Scaglietti, who felt that turning the sleek coupe into an open-air two-seat roadster was a natural. Paying careful attention to the lines, proportions, and the size of the revised driver's compartment, he then created a prototype. Ferrari was soon assaulted with a number of requests.

The model was designated the "365 GTS/4" (for *gran turismo spyder*), and it went into production in the second half of 1970. Approximately 125 were built over the next three years, and were especially popular in America's warmer climates; almost 80 percent of the production went to the States.

The Daytona Spyder proved to be the last hurrah for "old school" Ferrari, in which a talented artisan (Scaglietti) could approach another (Pininfarina) and have Ferrari sign off on the car's production. No sooner had Daytona Spyder production begun than America's safety and emissions regulations became more stringent, proving so complex and costly that Ferrari did not even attempt to legalize 365 GT4/BB, the mid-engine model that replaced the Daytona as Ferrari's flagship in 1974.

Still more drastic was the change in public

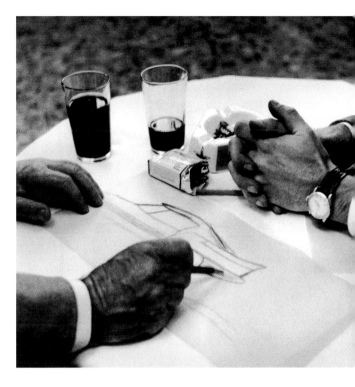

The hands of Battista Farina ("Pininfarina") and his son Sergio.

sentiment, which turned against cars like the Daytona Spyder. No longer were they seen as glamorous signs of success, but rather as representative of wasteful consumption in an age of diminishing resources. Global conferences on safety and commuter congestion weighed on people's minds, not sleek shapes and wind-in-the-hair fun.

As Daytona Spyder production wound down in 1973, *Automobile Year*'s Jean-Francis Held summed up this change in a poignant piece called "Twilight of the Goddesses." "All of us who are in love with beautiful motor cars are conscious of living something of a paradox," he observed. "At a time when, on all sides, the automobile is being reviled and accused of killing, of polluting, and stultifying, those of us who carry on nurturing our passion are beginning to feel like criminals on the run. Have we arrived at the crossroads? Are we experiencing, in short, the twilight of the goddesses we persist in adoring, come hell or high water?"

Indeed the world had. Several months after the article was published, the oil crisis hit. Companies such as Ferrari struggled to survive, and it would be another decade and more before machines like the Daytona Spyder would once again capture the world's imagination.

— WSG

1996 McLAREN F1

MANY OF HIS ADMIRERS believe
Gordon Murray to be incapable of
unoriginal thinking. The career of
this South African-born technical
virtuoso suggests it is not fulsome
praise. His race-car designs were always ingen-
ious and frequently brilliant. What didn't work
usually did not disappoint. A Bob Dylan fan
with rock star looks, Murray propelled his persona with the same relentless focus that
suffused his technical artistry and style. He
led, never followed. And when he put his hand
to the design of an automobile for the road, he
arrived at the ultimate super car of the waning
twentieth century.

In his native Durban, Murray was a one-
man design department. The son of a motor
mechanic and a graduate of the Natal Technical College, he became a race driver by building both his cars and the engines that went into
them because he couldn't afford an imported
racer of his own. In 1969, aware that a future
wouldn't happen for him in South Africa, Murray sold everything he owned to book passage
to England where he hoped to work for Lotus.
Instead he latched onto a job as a draftsman at
Brabham Cars and was a designer within three
years.

For the next sixteen years Murray designed
Formula and sports cars, the former most
memorably. His BT46 of 1977 replaced a conventional radiator with a body panel for car-
rying coolant, which, alas, didn't offer sufficient
surface-cooling capacity. In the subsequent
BT46B a huge fan drew in air at the rear of the
engine, which cooled the radiator and created

what came to be known as "ground-effects."
Brabham "Fan Car" was the name race enthusiasts coined. Authorities, fearing a superior-
ity that would make an event's outcome a boring certainty for the crowd, found a way to ban
it. Murray's 1986 design of the BT55, known
as the "Skateboard Brabham," asked a driver
to sit reclining with chin resting on chest.

Later in 1986 Murray left designing at Brabham for management at McLaren International. As technical director he worked to build
the team into a leading contender in Formula
One racing. More comfortable with solitary
work behind a drawing board, Murray found
supervising thirty employees unappealing.
Fortuitously, another job within the company
became available, for McLaren had decided to
join the very few automakers to attempt the
marketing of a cost-no-object super car. Once
again Murray was alone at the drafting board.

A technical tour de force, the McLaren F1
was a car of astonishing subtlety and sophistication. Most obvious of its distinctions was
the center position of the driver, flanked by
two passenger seats located a comfortable width
aft. As a college student in South Africa, Murray had doodled the F1's three-seat configuration in school notebooks. Anatomy had given
him the idea. The human form is widest at the
shoulders and hips; Murray's accommodating
overlap, which placed the center driver's seat
slightly forward of the seats flanking it, provided a three-passenger car in a remarkably
narrow envelope.

Compact on the outside, roomy on the inside
is an ideal rarely realized in automobile design.

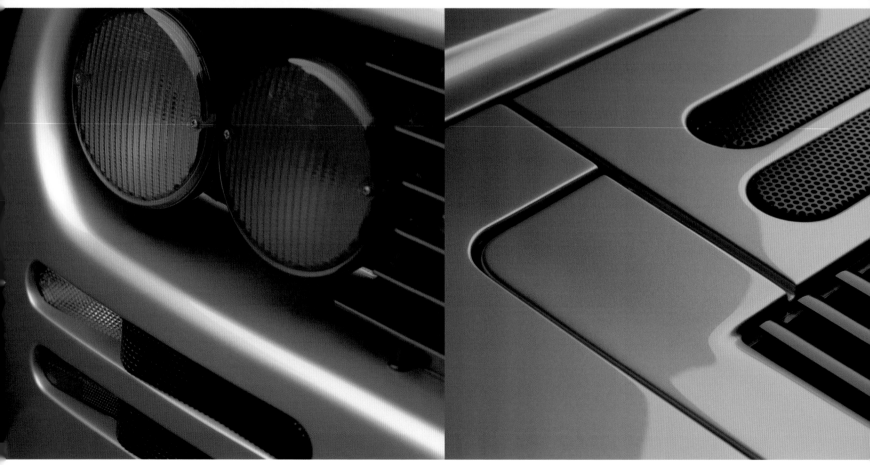

Despite the powerhouse engine under the hood —a 48-valve, 60-degree, 6.1-liter (366-cubic-inch), 627-horsepower all-aluminum V12 created for the car by BMW—the McLaren F1 measured only an inch longer than the contemporary Porsche 911. The center driving position allowed Murray to locate the driver's feet virtually at the front axle line. The six-speed transaxle was similarly truncated at the rear. Murray put luggage lockers on both sides aft of the doors in order that their contents not disturb the balance of the car.

"The world's first all carbon-composition production car," as McLaren called the F1, the entire package weighed a comparatively light 2,245 pounds. The F1's aerodynamics were exquisite. Murray mounted the engine's air intake scoop in the roof and incorporated a full ground-effects tray underneath where air entered beneath the front bumper and between flanking ports of the coolant radiators. To prevent the car nosing forward under deceleration, he incorporated a rear spoiler that popped up when the brakes were applied from high speed.

Boasting a phenomenal 500 lb./ft. of torque, top speed of the McLaren F1 was 231 mph. From a stop sign to 60 mph could be accomplished in 3.5 seconds. A few complained that visibility to the rear was poor, but no one could catch up to an F1 in any case. The view ahead from the driver's seat was a perfect panorama that contributed handsomely to the "master of my fate, captain of my soul" adrenaline rush that F1 drivers wrote rapturously about, whether testing the car's limits on a superhighway or rambling through picturesque small towns on the Continent, in old England, or in the New World.
— BRK

AMERICAN HERITAGE

1948 FORD "WOODY" STATION WAGON

THROUGH THE CENTURIES the body style for carriages that carried multiple passengers but that were not stage-coaches varied in designation, with such terms as Dutch wagon and German-town reflecting their adaptation from the old country. When the locomotive steamed its way onto the American scene, "depot hacks" taxied people to and from the railroad depot. The name "station wagon" was a logical evolution.

Early automobile makers adapted many horse-drawn carriage styles but ignored the station wagon. An automotive version could be had, however, by the simple expedient of buying a chassis and having a local carriage builder make one for you. Because the body style was regarded as a lowly utilitarian vehicle, the Model T Ford chassis was most often chosen by resorts, although one very fashionable establishment on the New Jersey coast ordered a mahogany-paneled body on a Cadillac chassis from Healey & Company, the posh New York City coachbuilder, in 1922.

In 1923 William Crapo Durant, who liked to gamble, became the first large American automobile manufacturer to catalogue a station wagon. Durant was the founder of General Motors who had lost control of the corporation

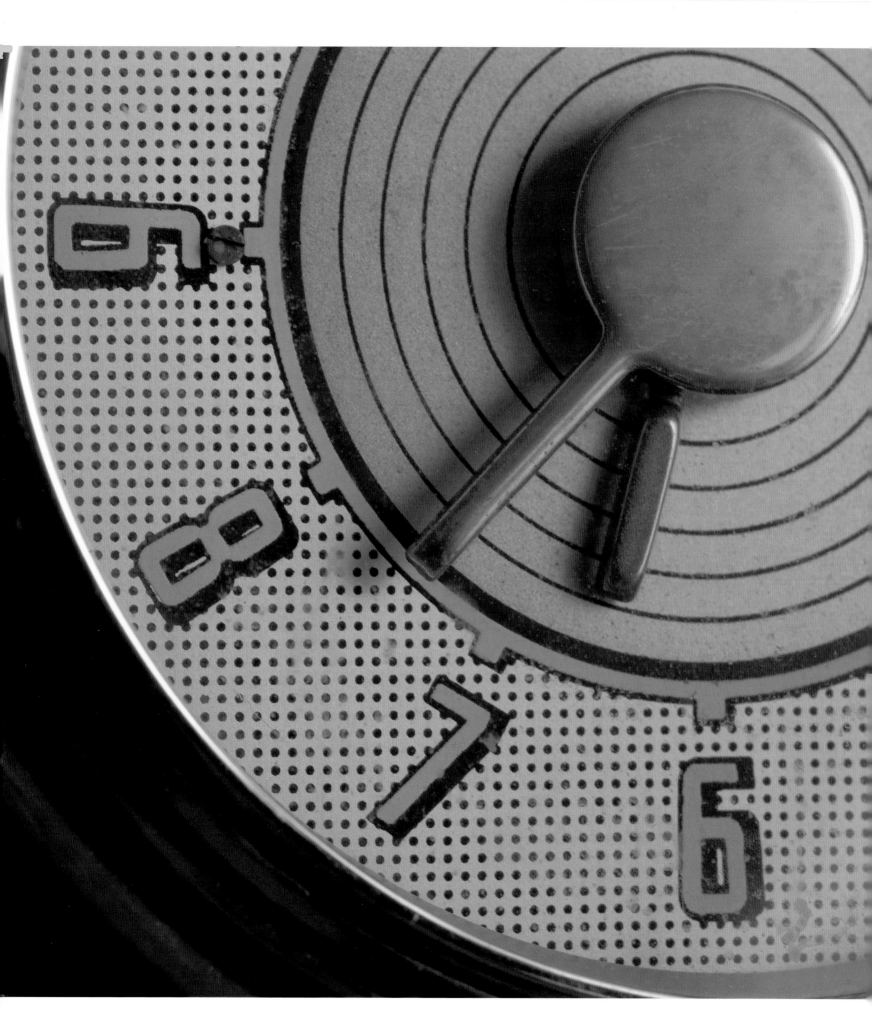

twice. When he began Durant Motors in the early twenties to compete with the colossus he had created, he lost another battle. His Star station wagon was gone by 1928, Durant Motors followed soon after the Great Depression began.

In its 1929 Model A catalogue, the Ford Motor Company first offered a station wagon, but sales of few more than eleven thousand through 1931 were pitiful compared to the more than one-and-one-quarter million standard Tudors (as Ford spelled its two-door models). The Mengel Furniture Company of Louisville, Kentucky, supplied the wood for the first Ford wagons until 1935 when Henry Ford began using his own maple and birch forests and the woodworking facilities at Iron Mountain, Michigan. Station wagon production remained more a Ford accommodation than a profit-maker through the thirties, but the company's vanguard position paid off handsomely after World War II when the wagon idea caught on with the populace. A "Woody" became the automotive Norman Rockwell. Few objects said Americana better.

The Ford Woody advertised in the *Saturday Evening Post*, November 1946. Part of the copy reads, "Here's an all-around car with polo field style . . . and sturdiness and space for light hauling, too."

Following Ford's lead, every major manufacturer jumped on the Woody wagon. In addition to its four-door Town & Country, Chrysler built a swank wood-paneled convertible coupe that became a favorite in Hollywood, both among the stars and on the screen. Of course, the Woody was impractical. The gluing, screwing, and varnishing required to put the body together was time intensive. The body style was often the most expensive in an automaker's catalogue, and the purchase was merely the beginning. Ford blithely admitted that the original finish was good for "about *one year* [Ford's emphasis] under ordinary circumstances." Thereafter the factory recommended annual stripping, sanding, bleaching, and revarnishing. Without proper maintenance, a Woody was prone to swelling, shrinking, creaking, and groaning.

Ford began to phase out its Woody wagon in 1948. The following year there was much more metal and far less wood. Ersatz wood paneling soon decorated the sides of new and thoroughly practical all-steel wagons. This dreadful idea was rather like putting a plastic apron on the mother serving Thanksgiving turkey in Rockwell's memorable painting.

— BRK

1951 WILLYS JEEP

IT STANDS four-square. No pretense, no guile. Equating beauty with honesty, the Army's Light Command and Reconnaissance Car is among the most gorgeous vehicles in the history of modern transportation—and one of the most important. The military designation was a mouthful, so GIs substituted Bantam, Blitz-Buggy, Peep, Gnat, and Jeep. Following its use in a *Washington Post* article, Jeep became the name evermore.

Necessity conceived the Jeep. The journey from paper to prototype was accomplished in a phenomenal forty-nine days because the American Bantam Company of Butler, Pennsylvania, was fighting for its life. Originally organized in 1930 to produce an American version of the English Austin, the company had foundered within a half decade, beginning its second life in 1938 under Roy Evans, a super salesman who believed that, evidence to the contrary, the American people stood ready to buy a small car provided one was produced that appealed to them. His friend, Count Alexis de Sakhnoffsky, offered to help. Arriving in the United States in 1928 from a career on the Continent designing custom-made coachwork, de Sakhnoffsky became quickly renowned as an automobile stylist of class and panache. The American Bantam he designed for expenses was a darling. But the American public still wasn't interested in a small car.

In 1939 Evans provided three Bantam roadsters to the Pennsylvania National Guard for use in maneuvers. Their performance gave Evans the confidence to bid for the Army contract for a four-wheel-drive scout car weighing no more than 1,300 pounds, roughly half the weight of the current Chevrolet. The contact seemed heaven-sent for a company whose specialty was small light cars. Bids were also going to such industry stalwarts as Ford and Willys-Overland, which did not daunt Roy Evans.

Chief engineer Karl Probst was daunted, however, by the two days he had to design a car to meet the bid deadline. When the final specs from the Army arrived, there was pandemonium in Butler. Minimum horsepower had been raised from twenty to forty, too much for the Bantam's transmission and axles. "We'll have to jack up the horn button so you can design a new car under it," Bantam president Frank Fenn lamented to Probst. Now ready for the challenge, Karl said they could produce drawings faster than the competition. Bantam won the contract, and was given seven days to produce the product.

"We know you have no engineering department left," Major Herbert Lawes, purchasing officer for Camp Holabird, wired. "Probst will have to find one quickly." In Detroit Karl secured the services of three engineers, Fenn found a fourth. Forty-seven days later, sixteen people who had made it happen crowded around the car as someone yelled, "Get a Kodak."

The forty-ninth day was a ninety-degree Monday in Butler as Probst and a colleague drove the car that would be the Jeep to Camp Holabird. Major Lawes had tested every vehicle the Army had bought in the last two decades and flogged this one over all manner of terrain, declaring afterward that "this unit will make history." Then came the rub. The Army

wanted Jeeps faster than the small facilities in Butler could make them. Ford and Willys-Overland got the manufacturing contracts to produce over 600,000 Jeeps, American Bantam less than three thousand.

General George C. Marshall called the Jeep "America's greatest contribution to modern warfare." Wrote Ernie Pyle in the midst of operations in the European theater, "I don't think we could continue the war without the Jeep. It does everything." As the American Bantam Company withered and died in Butler, Jeeps went everywhere in combat from Salerno to the Burma Road.

With peace, the thousands of Jeeps left overseas helped put on wheels those undeveloped nations not previously reached by the Model T Ford. Back home, however, it was a victor now on the verge of being vanquished. The Jeep would probably have remained government issue save for the same matter of necessity that conceived it in the first place. The industry's return to the business of building automobiles had been greeted euphorically by an Ameri-

can public deprived of new cars since shortly after Pearl Harbor. The rush to purchase was on. Prior to the war, Willys-Overland had not produced its own coachwork, farming that chore out to several large body-building companies. Now, to its chagrin, W-O's traditional sources of supply chose to take on the massive orders arriving from GM, Ford, and Chrysler instead. A metal fabricating company willing to work for Willys finally was found but unfortunately its specialty was household appliances that did not require the compound curves and raised

accent lines of the prototypical American auto-mobile. W-O could have any body it wanted so long as it was simple and had slab sides.

That limiting factor persuaded Willys-Over-land to leave the passenger car arena for the commercial one, hiring designer Brooks Stevens to develop station wagons and pickup trucks on the basis of the Jeep. The Jeep itself was painted colors bearing no resemblance to olive drab and was sent to market too. Beating swords into plowshares became a literal fact. The civilian version of the Jeep was advertised

as a help-mate for farmers for "operating hammer mills, buzz saws, silo blowers, sprayers and power mowers." Ultimately a small version was created for the generation that discovered a Jeep was fun.

The metamorphosis from tool of war to tool of peace to the luxury sport utility vehicle that the Jeep is today has been extraordinary. Wise was the fellow who had the foresight in the midst of World War II to register the name as a trademark. There was just one glitch. Willys also advertised itself as the creator of the Jeep. In 1948 the corporation received a "cease and desist" order from the Federal Trade Commission, which declared that inventive honor belonged in Butler. The American Bantam Company was now largely forgotten and so was the man who had designed a landmark car from a horn button. In 1963 Karl Probst died by his own hand, a blueprint of the Jeep wrapped around him.

— BRK

A Willys Jeep advertisement touting the vehicle's post-war utility on the American farm.

HISTORIES

by Mark Reinwald, with additional information by Marcel Massini

Blower Bentley

Built 1929
Chassis #HR3976
One of five built
One of only two short wheelbase cars

OWNERSHIP HISTORY

1929: Hon. Dorothy Paget, England
1931: Unknown, France
1980s: Anthony Bramford, England
1988: Ralph Lauren

RACE HISTORY

1930: Double Twelve Race, Brooklands, driver Benjafield, did not finish (rear axle problem)
1930: Le Mans, drivers Benjafield and Ramponi, did not finish (blown piston)
1930: Irish Grand Prix, driver Birkin, 4th place
1930: Tourist Trophy Race, driver Birkin, did not finish (crashed)
1930: French Grand Prix, driver Birkin, 2nd place
1930: 500 Miles Race, Brooklands, place
1932: Le Mans, drivers Pierre Brousselet and J. Trevoux, did not finish
1933: Le Mans, drivers Trevoux and Gas, did not finish (crashed)

Mercedes-Benz "Count Trossi" SSK

Built 1930 (chassis)
Chassis #36038

OWNERSHIP HISTORY

1930: Chassis sent to Tokyo sales agent in February, returned to the factory in September.
October sent to Mercedes-Benz sales agent Carlo Saporiti in Milan
1932: Count Carlo Felice Trossi, Italy, as a chassis. Coachwork privately commissioned to his own design. Resold/exchanged with friends several times in Italy.
1950: Ricardo Polledo, Argentina
1952: Charlie Stitch, U.S.A.
1954: Carter Schaub, U.S.A.
1963: Raymond Jones, U.S.A.
1975: Anthony Bamford, U.K.
1980: Thomas Perkins, U.S.A.
1988: Ralph Lauren

RACE HISTORY

None

Mercedes-Benz 300SL Gullwing Coupe

Built 1955
Chassis #198.040-5500386
Built by Mercedes-Benz Sindelfingen

OWNERSHIP HISTORY

1955: AGAM BV, Netherlands
1983: Ralph Lauren

RACE HISTORY

None

Mercedes-Benz 300SL Roadster

Built 1958
Chassis #198.042-8500208
Built by Mercedes-Benz Sindelfingen

OWNERSHIP HISTORY

1958: Unknown
1979: John Mann, U.S.A.
1982: Larry Pfitzenmaier through Thorobred Motorcars
1983: Ralph Lauren

RACE HISTORY

None

Alfa Romeo Monza 8C 2300

Built 1931
Chassis #2111043

OWNERSHIP HISTORY

1931: Alfa Romeo
1932: Jean Pierre Wimille, France
1933: Giovanni Battaglia, Italy
About 1937: Cristofo Biggi, Eritrea, Africa
1943: Found by British Army in Ethiopia
1943: T. R. Africa
194?: Bunbary (Naval Engineer Lieutenant), Africa
1950: Franciosi, Africa
1952: Gaetano Barone, Africa
1962: Joel Finn, U.S.A.
196?: William Irwin, U.S.A.
196?: Ray Jones, U.S.A.
1966: Stanford Landell, U.S.A.
1970s: Stephen Griswold, U.S.A.
1980s: Klaus Werner, Germany
1980s: Ekhart Berg, Germany
1988: Ralph Lauren

RACE HISTORY

1932: Pontedecimo-Giovi, driver Wimille, 6th place in class
1932: Lorraine Grand Prix, driver Wimille, 1st place
1932: French Grand Prix, driver Wimille, did not finish (ran out of fuel)
1932: Dieppe Grand Prix, driver Wimille, crashed
1932: Commings Grand Prix, driver Wimille, did not finish
1932: Antibes Grand Prix, driver Wimille, crashed
1933: Pau Grand Prix, driver Wimille, practiced only, did not start
1933: La Turbie Hill Climb, driver Wimille, 1st place
1933: Monaco Grand Prix, driver Wimille, did not finish
1933: Circuito di Firenze, driver Battaglia, 2nd place

1933: Pontedecimo-Giovi, driver Battaglia, 7th place racing car class

1933: Coppa Ciano, driver Battaglia, 5th place

1933: Stelvio Hill Climb, driver Battaglia, 2nd place racing car class, 6th overall

1933: Moncenisio Hill Climb, driver Battaglia, 2nd place

1933: Ticino Hill Climb, driver Battaglia, 2nd racing car class

1934: Targa Florio, driver Battaglia,

1934: Targa Vesuvio, driver Battaglia, 3rd place

1934: Varese Campo dei Fiori, driver Battaglia, crashed

1934: Mille Miglia, drivers Battaglia and Bianchi, 4th place

1935: Varese Campo dei Fiori, driver Battaglia, 3rd place

1935: Varese Circuito, driver Battaglia, 4th place

1935: Mille Miglia, drivers Battaglia and Tufanelli, 3rd place

1938: Asmara, Africa, driver possibly Biggi

Alfa Romeo 8C 2900 Mille Miglia

Built 1938
Chassis #412030
Coachwork by Carrozzeria Touring, First of four cars built

OWNERSHIP HISTORY

1938: Retained by the factory Racing Team "Alfa Corse"

1939: Marchese Giovanni Cornaggio, Italy
Alfa Romeo
Count Carlo Felice Trossi, Italy

1940: Vercelli, Italy

1948: Tommy Lee, U.S.A.

1951: Phil Hill, U.S.A.

1953: James Magin, U.S.A.

1955: Brooks Stevens, U.S.A.

1982: Bill Serri, U.S.A.

2004: Ralph Lauren

RACING HISTORY

1938: XXII Mille Miglia, race 142, drivers Pintacuda and Mambelli, 2nd place overall
Colli Torinese Hill Climb, race 142, driver Mario Tadini, 1st place overall
Parma Berceto Hill Climb, race 166, driver Emilio Villoresi, 1st place overall
Pontedecimo-Giovi Hill Climb, race 112, driver Nino Farina, 1st place overall

1949: Pikes Peak Hill Climb USA, race 2, driver Mack Hellings, fastest time of day, later disputed

Watkins Glen Grand Prix, race 40, driver Mal Ord, did not finish

1951: Del Monte Handicap, race 2, driver Phil Hill, 1st place
Pebble Beach Cup, race 2, driver Hill, 4th place

Bugatti Type 59 Grand Prix

Built 1933
Chassis #59122
Engine #1
First of eight built

OWNERSHIP HISTORY

1933: Bugatti (works car)

1935: Lindsay Eccles, England

1938: Jack Lemon Burton, England

1943: Atkins, England

1943: W.B. Hindes, England

1946: Rodney Clark, Continental Cars, England

1947: Ivan Carr, England

1953: Bob Roberts, England

1959: Denis de Ferranti, England

1986: Ralph Lauren

RACE HISTORY

1933: Belgian Grand Prix, driver Achille Varzi, practice only

1933: Spanish Grand Prix, San Sebastian, driver Varzi, 4th place

1934: Monaco Grand Prix, driver Tazio Nuvolari, 5th place

1934: Tripoli Grand Prix, driver Antonio Brivio, did not finish (engine blew)

1934: French Grand Prix, Montlhery, drivers Nuvolari and Wimille, did not finish (gearbox)

1934: Belgian Grand Prix, Spa, driver Brivio, 2nd place and set new lap record

1934: Coppa Acerbo, Pescara, driver Brivio, 3rd place

1934: Italian Grand Prix, Monza, driver Brivio, practice only

1934: Spanish Grand Prix, San Sebastian, driver Nuvolari, 3rd place

1934: Czech Grand Prix, Brno, driver Robert Benoist, did not finish

1935: Brooklands, race 3, 4, 9, driver Lindsay Eccles, unplaced, 3rd, and 2nd place

1935: International Trophy, Brooklands, driver Eccles, did not finish (torque arm)

1935: Hill Climb, Shelsley Walsh, driver Eccles, non-started

1935: Mannin Moar, Isle of Man, driver Eccles, did not finish (transmission)

1935: B. E. Trophy, Brooklands, driver Eccles, non-started

1935: Senior Handicap, Donington, driver Eccles, 1st place

1935: Dieppe Grand Prix, driver Eccles, engine blew in practice

1935: BOC Speed Trials, Lewes, driver Eccles, 2nd place

1935: Speed Trials, Brighton, driver Eccles, 2nd place

1935: Hill Climb, Shelsley, driver Eccles, 1st place in class

1935: Donington Grand Prix, drivers Eccles and Pat Fairfield, 6th place

1935: Brooklands, races 5 and 8, driver Eccles, non-started

1936: B. E. Trophy, Donington, driver Eccles, 6th place

1936: International Trophy, Brooklands, driver Eccles, did not finish (ignition)

1936: Brooklands, race 4, driver Eccles, non-started

1936: Hill Climb, Shelsley Walsh, driver Eccles, 1st place in class

1936: BOC Speed Trials, Lewes, driver Eccles, 1st place in class

1939: Hill Climb, BOC Prescott, driver Jack Lemon Burton, unplaced

1939: Hill Climb, Walsh, driver Burton, unplaced

1939: Hill Climb, BOC Prescott, driver Burton, unplaced

1939: Brooklands, race 1, driver Burton, unplaced

1946: Hill Climb, BOC Prescott, drivers Rodney Clarke and Louis Giron, non-started

1946: Hill Climb, BOC Prescott, drivers Clarke and Giron, unplaced

1947: Hill Climb, BOC Prescott, driver Mike Oliver, unplaced

1955: Hill Climb, BOC Prescott, driver Bob Roberts, unplaced

1955: Hill Climb, BOC Prescott, driver Roberts, unplaced

1957: Hill Climb, BOC Prescott, driver Roberts, unplaced

1958: Hill Climb, BOC Prescott, driver Roberts, unplaced

1958: Hill Climb, BOC Prescott, driver Roberts, non-started

Bugatti Type 57SC Gangloff Drop Head Coupe

Built 1937
Chassis #57563
Coachwork by Gangloff
One of two Gangloff Drop Heads built

1937: Sold as a chassis to Philippe Levy, Strasbourg, France
Coachwork privately contracted with Carrozzeria Gangloff, design # 3747
1940: G. Docine, France
1948: Vivian Corradini, U.S.A.
1951: Robert Fergus, U.S.A.
1986: Ralph Lauren, U.S.A.

RACE HISTORY

None

Bugatti Type 57SC Atlantic Coupe

Built 1938
Chassis #57591
Coachwork by Bugatti
Third of three built

OWNERSHIP HISTORY

1938: Richard B. Pope, U.K.
1966: Barrie Price, U.K.
1976: Anthony Bamford, U.K.
1980: Thomas Perkins, U.S.A.
1988: Ralph Lauren

RACE HISTORY

None

Morgan Plus Four

Built 1954
Chassis #3274

OWNERSHIP HISTORY

1954: Not known
1983: Purchased from Donald Simpkins by Ralph Lauren

RACE HISTORY

None

Jaguar XK120

Built 1950
Chassis #660043
One of six factory works cars
The only XK120 works car to stay under the ownership of Jaguar; the others were sold to private owners to race

OWNERSHIP HISTORY

1950: Jaguar
1960s: Rhoddy Harvey-Bailey, England
1985: Sold by Dan Margulies, London, to Ralph Lauren

RACE HISTORY

1950: Targa Florio, driver Clemente Biondetti, did not finish (blown engine)
1950: Mille Miglia, driver Biondetti, 8th place overall
1950: Parma-Poggio di Berceto Road Race, driver Biondetti, 3rd place
1950: Giro dell'Umbria, driver Biondetti, crashed
1960s: Raced by Rhoddy Harvey-Bailey, England

Jaguar XKD

Chassis #505/601
Built 1955/56
First of six long-nose cars built in 1955
One of only ten long-nose D-types built
First Jaguar (601) to have Lucas Fuel Injection (later changed to Webers)
Crashed at 1958 Le Mans, was rebuilt at the factory using many XKD505 parts

OWNERSHIP HISTORY

1956: Jaguar
1957–58: Duncan Hamilton
1950s: John Coundley
Jim Rodgers
Peter Sargent
1964: Patricia Coundley
1960s: Anthony Bamford
1982: Bob Roberts
1983: Adrian Hamilton
1985: Ralph Lauren

RACE HISTORY

1956: Reims, drivers Hawthorn and Frere, 2nd place
1956: Sebring, drivers Hawthorn and Titterington, race 8, did not finish (brakes)
1956: Nürburgring, drivers Hawthorn and Titterington, did not finish
1957: Le Mans, drivers Hamilton and Gregory, race 4, 6th place overall
1958: Le Mans, driver Hamilton and Bureb, crashed
1964: Antwerp Speed Trials, driver Patricia Coundley (at 161.278 mph, she became the "fastest woman in Europe")

Jaguar XKSS

Built 1956 as XKD
Chassis #XKD533

1958 Changed to XKSS at factory for Pierre Chemin
One of eighteen built

OWNERSHIP HISTORY

1956: Delacroix, France
1956: Monnoyeur, France
1957: Pierre Chemin, France
1970: Dr. Phillippe Renault, France
1988: David Cottingham, England
1989: Kerry Manolas, Australia
1989: Ralph Lauren

RACE HISTORY

1957: Forez Six Hour Race

Ferrari 375 Plus

Built 1954
Chassis #0398 AM
Built by Pininfarina
Fifth of five built

OWNERSHIP HISTORY

1954: Enrique Diaz Saenz Valiente, Argentina
1956: Luis Milan, Argentina
1959: Advertised for sale by Dr. Vincente Alvarez, Buenos Aires
1960s: Augustin Somonte, Buenos Aires
1970: Alain de Cadenet, England
1978: Ernesto P. Dillon, Buenos Aires
1983: Ed Jurist's Vintage Car Store, Nyack, New York
1984: Don Walker, Dallas, Texas
1985: Ralph Lauren

RACE HISTORY

1955: 1000 kms of Buenos Aires, race 4, drivers Valiente and Ibanez, 1st place overall
1955: Circuito del Parco, driver Valiente, 1st place overall
1955: Grand Prix Sport di Otono, driver Valiente, 2nd place
1955: Gran Premio Independencia, driver Valiente, 1st place
1955: Gran Premio Inverno at Buenos Aires, driver Valiente, 1st place
1955: El Bosque event, driver Valiente, 1st place
1955: Gran Prix Tres Arroyos, driver Valiente, 1st place
1956: 1000 km of Buenos Aires, race 45, drivers Valiente and Jorge Camano, did not finish
1957: Circuito di Buenos Aires, race 23, driver Milan
1958: El Penon race, driver Milan
1959: Gran Premio Primavera at Buenos Aires, race 1, driver Milan

1967: Premio Apertura Formula Libre race at Buenos Aires, race# 32, driver Cesar Rivero, 1st place overall, front slightly damaged

Ferrari 250 Testa Rossa

Built 1958
Chassis #0734
Body by Scaglietti
Fourteenth of thirty-four built

OWNERSHIP HISTORY

1958: Frederick H. Gibbs, New York
1978: Paul Pappalardo, Connecticut
1985: Albert Obrist, Switzerland
1985: Ralph Lauren

RACE HISTORY

None

Ferrari 250 TR 61 Spyder Fantuzzi

Built 1961
Chassis #0792
One of two cars built

OWNERSHIP HISTORY

1961: Ferrari
1961: 9/30 Count Giovanni Volpi di Misurata, Italy
1968: S.A.S. Berghiun, Italy
1985: Ralph Lauren, USA

RACE HISTORY

1961: Sebring, drivers Phil Hill and Oliver Gendebien, 1st place
1961: LeMans, drivers Pedro and Ricardo Rodriguez, did not finish (blown engine)
1961: Governor's Trophy, driver Gram Hill, 5th place
1961: Boxing Day, Brands Hatch, driver Graham Hill, 1st place
1962: Sebring, drivers Joakim Bonnier and Lucien Bianchi, 1st place
1962: ADAC 100kms, Nurburgring, drivers Maria and Vaccarella, did not finish (accident)
1962: LeMans, drivers Joakim Bonnier and Dan Gurney, did not finish (rear hub)
1962: Brands Hatch, driver Bonnier, 3rd place
1962: Ollon-Villars hillclimb, driver Nino Vaccarella
1963: ADAC 1000kms, Nurburgring, drivers Maglioli and Abate, 3rd place
1963: GT and sport cars, Reims, driver Abate, 1st place

1963: Auvergne Trophy, driver Bandini, 1st place
1963: Bank Holiday, Brands Hatch, driver Abate, did not finish (lost wheel)

Ferrari 250 GTO

Built 1962
Chassis #3987
Body built by Scaglietti
Twenty-first of thirty-six built

OWNERSHIP HISTORY

1962: Luigi Chinetti's NART racing team, U.S.A.
1962: John Mecom, Jr. (Mecom Racing Team), U.S.A.
1963: Otto Zipper Motors, U.S.A.
1965: S. Mitchell, U.S.A.
1971: Alain de Cadenet, England
1972: Stuart H. Baumgard, U.S.A.
1978: Nessim Gaon and Spencer Stillman, U.S.A.
1983: Don Walker, U.S.A.
1985: Ralph Lauren

RACE HISTORY

1962: Paris 1000 kilometers, Linas-Montlhery, drivers Pedro and Ricardo Rodriguez, 1st place
1962: Governor's Trophy, Bahamas Speed Week, driver Rodger Penske
1962: Tourist Trophy "Preliminary," Bahamas Speed Week, driver Penske, 1st place
1962: Tourist Trophy, Bahamas Speed Week, driver Penske, 1st place
1963: Three-Hour Daytona Continental, driver Penske, 2nd place
1963: 12 Hours of Sebring, drivers Penske and Augie Pabst, 4th place overall, 1st in class
1963: USRRC GT event Pensacola, driver Penske, 1st place
1963: USRRC Road America 500 Miles, drivers Penske and Pabst, 8th place overall, 2nd in class
1963: SCCA Races Lynndale Farms, WI, driver Pabst, 2nd place overall, 1st in class
1963: LA Times Grand Prix, Riverside, driver Richie Ginther, 5th place
1964: LA Times Grand Prix, Riverside, driver Ginther, 5th place
1973: Ferrari Owners Club, U.S.A., Hill Climb, CA, driver Claudio Zampolli, 4th place

Porsche 550 Spyder

Built 1955
Chassis #5500061
Sixty-first of ninety built

OWNERSHIP HISTORY

1984: Purchased by Ralph Lauren from Everett Singer

RACE HISTORY

None

Porsche RSK

Built 1959
Chassis #718-009
Ninth of thirty-four built

OWNERSHIP HISTORY

1988: Bought by Ralph Lauren from Richard Roth

RACE HISTORY

Unknown

Aston Martin DB5 Volante

Built 1965
Chassis #DB5C 1910 R
One of 123 built

OWNERSHIP HISTORY

1965: Paul Hamlyn Holdings, England
1965–80s: Owners unknown
1983: Sold by Coys Ltd., England to Ralph Lauren

RACE HISTORY

None

Ferrari 250 GT SWB Berlinetta Scaglietti

Built 1960
Chassis #
Alloy body by Scaglietti
Thirty-first of 165 built

OWNERSHIP HISTORY

1960: Jorge de Moura Pinheiro, Portugal
1961: Horacio Macedo, Portugal
1964: Antonio Simoes Madeira, Portugal
1970: Dr. Joao de Lacerda, Portugal
1976: Edward H. Swart, Holland
1984: Donald R. Walker, Texas
1986: Ralph Lauren

1960: Supporting GT event for the X Portuguese Grand Prix, driver Pinheiro, 1st place

1960: Grand Prix of Angola, driver Pinheiro/Correia

1961: Circuit of Alverca, driver Macedo, 1st place

1961: Circuito Vila do Conde, driver Macedo, 2nd place

1961: Rampa de Santa Cristina Hill Climb, driver Macedo, 1st place

1961: Falperra Hill Climb, driver Macedo, 1st place

1962: Rallye de Montanha, driver Macedo, 1st place

1962: Circuit of Portugal, driver Macedo, 1st place

1962: Grand Rallye do Sporting, driver Macedo, 1st place

1962: International Tour of Madeira Island, driver Macedo, 1st place

1962: Rallye San Pedro de Noel, driver Macedo, 1st place

1962: Arrabida Hill Climb, driver Macedo, 1st place

1962: Rallye de San Martino, driver Macedo, 1st place

1962: Rampa de Santa Cristina Hill Climb, driver Macedo, 1st place

1963: Santa Cristina do Couto, driver Macedo, 1st place

1963: AC Portugal Rallye, driver Macedo, 1st place

1963: Rallye Internacional do ACP Algarve-Estoril, driver Macedo, 1st place

1963: Coppa d'Oro, driver Macedo, 1st place

1963: Rallye de Montanha, driver Macedo, 1st place

1963: Rallye San Pedro de Noel, driver Macedo, 1st place

1963: Grand Rallye do Sporting, driver Macedo, 1st place

1963: International Tour of Madeira Island, driver Macedo, 1st place

1963: Coppa de La Pena, driver Macedo, 1st place

1963: Rallye de San Martino, driver Macedo, 1st place

1963: International Tour of Portugal, driver Macedo, 1st place

1964: Rallye Internacional do ACP Algarve-Estoril, driver Macedo, disqualified

1964: Volta ao Minho, driver Macedo, 1st place

1965: Taca Camara Municipal de Cascais, driver Antonio Madeira, did not finish

1969: Montes Claros, driver Casteliano Junior, 7th place

1976: 7/18 Zandvoort, driver Swart, 1st place

1976: 8/15 Zandvoort, driver Swart, 1st place

1977: 4/11 Zandvoort, driver Swart, 2nd place

1977: 5/30 Zandvoort, driver Swart, 2nd place

1977: Donington Park, driver Swart, 2nd place

1978: 4/16 Zandvoort, driver Swart, 2nd place

1978: 5/15 Zandvoort, driver Swart, 2nd place

1978: 6/24 Zandvoort, driver Swart, did not finish (engine)

1978: Nürburgring, driver Swart, 2nd place in class

1978: Zolder, driver Swart, did not finish (half shaft broke)

1979: 8/5 Zolder, driver Swart, 1st place

1979: Spa-Francorchamps, driver Swart, 1st place

1979: 10/7 Zolder, driver Swart, 1st place

1980: 4/27 Zandvoort, driver Swart, 1st place

1980: 5/18 driver Swart, 1st place

1981: Monterey Historic Races, driver Swart, 2nd place

1981: VARA races at Riverside, driver Swart, 1st place

1982: LA Times/Toyota Grand Prix at Riverside, driver Swart, 1st place

1982: Monterey Historic Races, driver Swart, 1st place

1982: VARA races Riverside, driver Swart, 1st place

1983: Laguna Seca, driver Swart, 1st place

1983: Monterey Historic Races, driver Swart 1st place

Ferrari 250 GT Spyder California

Built 1960
Chassis #2167GT

OWNERSHIP HISTORY

1960: Massimo Auregli, Italy

1962: Wolfgang Seidel, Germany

1962: Gunther Lohstraeter, Germany

1967: Andre Cesar Carre, France

1985: Sassocar Srl., Italy

1985: Pier Paolo Apicella, Italy

1985: Emilianauto SpA, Italy

1985: Ralph Lauren

RACE HISTORY

1961: Rossfeld Hill Climb, driver Lohstraeter, 1st place in GT class

1962: Coupe de Bruxelles, driver Lohstraeter

1962: Oberschleissheim Airfield Race

Ferrari 250LM

Built 1964
Chassis #6321
Body by Scaglietti
Thirty-first of thirty-two built

OWNERSHIP HISTORY

1964: David McKay (Scuderia Veloce), Australia

1984: Ralph Lauren

RACE HISTORY

1965: Sandown Park, driver Spencer Martin, 1st place

1965: 3/1 Longford, driver Martin, 1st place

1965: Lakeside, driver Martin, 1st place

1965: 3/27 Longford, driver Martin, 1st place

1965: Moont Panorama, driver Martin, 1st place

1965: RAAC Trophy, Warwick Farm, driver Martin, 5th place

1965: 5/16 Warwick Farm, driver Martin, 1st place

1965: Perth Six Hours, driver Martin, 1st place

1965: Lakeside, driver Martin, 3rd place

1965: 8/7 Warwick Farm, driver Martin, 2nd place

1965: 9/19 Warwick Farm, driver Martin, 1st place

1965: 9/26 Warwick Farm, driver Martin, 2nd place

1965: Catalina Park, driver Martin, 1st place

1965: Australian Tourist Trophy, Lakeside, driver Martin, 3rd place

1965: 12/5 Warwick Farm, driver Martin, 2nd place

1966: Christchurch, driver Martin, 1st place

1966: Surfers Paradise Twelve Hours, drivers Jackie Stewart and Andy Buchanan, 1st place

1967: Surfers Paradise Twelve Hours, drivers Greg Cusack and Bill Brown, 1st place

1968: Surfers Paradise Six Hours, drivers Leo and Ian Geoghegan, 1st place

1984: Monterey Historic Races, driver Martin, 3rd place

Ferrari 275 P2/3 Spyder Drogo

Built 1965
Chassis #0826
Originally a 3.3-liter 275 P2, upgraded later into a 4.4-liter 365 P3

1965: Ferrari NART Team

1965: Colonel Ronnie Hoare, Maranello Concessionaires Racing Team, England

1966: David A. Clarke, England

1985: Paul E. Vestey, England

1988: Ralph Lauren

RACE HISTORY

1965: Daytona Continental 200 kilometers, drivers John Surtees and Pedro Rodriguez, did not finish (axle failure)

1965: Lemans Twenty-four Hours, drivers David Piper and Joakim Bonnier, did not finish (hole in exhaust manifold)

1965: Reims Twelve Hours, drivers Surtees and Mike Parks, 2nd place

1965: Austrian Sports Car Grand Prix, driver Parks, 2nd place

1965: Guards International Trophy, Brands Hatch, driver Parks, 6th place 1st heat, 8th place 2nd heat

1966: Le Mans Twenty-four Hours, drivers Richard Attwood and Piper, did not finish (water pump)

Ferrari 275 GTB/4 NART Spyder

Built 1967
Chassis #10219
One of ten built

OWNERSHIP HISTORY

1967: Unknown

1984: Ralph Lauren

RACE HISTORY

None

Ferrari 365 GTS/4 Daytona Spyder

Built 1973
Chassis #16499
Built by Scaglietti
One of 125 built

OWNERSHIP HISTORY

1973: Bonnie Gallogly, New Jersey

1981: Rodney Lee Propps, South Carolina

1984: Foreign Cars Italia, North Carolina

1984: Ralph Lauren

RACE HISTORY

None

McLaren F1

Built 1996
Chassis #SA9AB5AC8T1048055
Fifty-five of seventy-five total production cars

OWNERSHIP HISTORY

1996: Ralph Lauren

RACE HISTORY

None

Ford "Woody" Station Wagon

Built 1948
Chassis #899A2080585

OWNERSHIP HISTORY

Before 1990: Robert S. Ingraham, other owners unknown

1990: Ralph Lauren

RACE HISTORY

None

GLOSSARY

barchetta
An open Italian two-seat sports car, typically (but not always) devoid of creature comforts.

berlinetta
Meaning "little sedan" in Italian, it usually refers to a car with a *fastback* body.

bhp
An abbreviation of "brake horsepower," it is a means by which to measure the power of an engine. The term is used because an engine's output is measured by a dynometer, or "brake."

blower
See *supercharger*.

cabriolet
An open car that typically has a folding top and four seats.

carrozzeria
An Italian firm that designs and/or makes bodies for cars.

cc
The abbreviation for "cubic centimeters," which is used as a measurement for engines.

chassis
The car minus its body, accessories, and trim. The frame and all its operating parts, such as the suspension and brakes. Each chassis is given a unique number by its manufacturer; this number is then used by the company and historians to keep track of the car.

coachbuilding
The craft of designing and/or manufacturing car bodies.

coachbuilder
A person or firm that designs and/or manufacturers car bodies; see *carrozzeria*.

coupe
A two- or four-seat car with two doors and a hardtop. Derived from the French word *couper*, "to cut."

cylinder
The hollow structure inside an engine block in which the piston travels.

straight-eight engine
An engine with eight cylinders arranged in two parallel banks of four cylinders each. In a V8 engine, the two cylinder banks form a "V" in shape, rather than being parallel.

drivetrain
The components of a car that transmit power; these include items such as the clutch, gearbox, and driveshaft.

fastback
A car body in which the roof slopes downward in one continuous line that ends at the rear of the car.

flange
A protruding rim or edge that typically strengthens an object, attaches one object to another, or holds the object in place.

Formula One
The ultimate form of motorsport. The cars for a Formula One race usually use the most advanced technology. Formula One cars are open-wheel racers, i.e. the wheels are completely exposed and out a distance from the car's body.

Formula Two
Similar to Formula One but the open-wheel cars are less powerful.

Gran Turismo
Also known as a "GT," or a "grand touring" car, it is a car that offers superior comfort and performance, so that when its occupants arrive at their destination they feel as refreshed as when they left.

Grand Prix
See Formula One.

Le Mans
Named after a town in France, it is the world's most famous and prestigious race. The race's duration is twenty-four hours, and it is held annually in mid-June.

monocoque structure
A type of body construction in which the body panels are stressed members that become part of the supporting structure. Nature's perfect monocoque is the egg.

production car
A car typically produced in large quantities.

performance car
A car that offers high performance.

roadster
The term originated in pre-World War II America and refers to an open car without windows. Today it is most closely associated with an open two-seat sports car, typically of British origin.

spyder (spider)
An open two-seat sports car of Italian origin. Spyders have creature comforts not found in the more rudimentary *barchetta*.

supercharger
A pump that forces air into the cylinders, making the pressure inside greater than that of the atmosphere. This pressure causes the engine to burn more fuel and thus deliver more power. A supercharger is also called a "blower."

suspension
Components such as shock absorbers, springs, and linkages that suspend a car's body, frame, drivetrain, and engine above the wheels.

touring car
An open car with four or five seats that has a folding (collapsing) top. The term is used most commonly with pre-WWI cars.

ACKNOWLEDGMENTS

FOR THEIR HELP in organizing and advising about the exhibition that formed the basis for this book, the Museum is deeply grateful to several individuals. First and foremost, we thank Ralph Lauren for embracing the idea of the exhibition early on and making his amazing collection available for display. For their assistance in an array of logistical issues, we are likewise indebted to several members of the staff at Polo Ralph Lauren, including Ali Bovis, Mary Randolph Carter, Bette-Ann Gwathmey, David Lauren, Nancy E. S. Murray, and Alfredo Paredes. We also wish to thank Merrill Lynch for its support of the exhibition.

From the MFA's staff, I am personally grateful to Malcolm Rogers, Ann and Graham Gund Director, and Kathryn Getchell, Deputy Director for Curatorial Administration, for their valuable support of this project since its inception. Other Museum staff members who have played keyed roles in organizing and presenting the actual exhibition include Arthur Beale, Jennifer Bose, Ellen Bragalone, Keith Crippen, Kelly Gifford, Dawn Griffin, David Geldart, Alex Huff, Patricia Loiko, Barbara Martin, Marlie L. McManus, William McAvoy, Janet O'Donoghue, Jaime Roark, Gilian Shallcross, John Stanley, and Jennifer Weissman. Several members of the MFA's Department of Publications, along with consultants and interns, deserve particular mention for their skill and finesse in bringing this handsome book to fruition. Included here are Denise Bergman, Kristin Caulfield, Jenell Forschler, Susan Marsh, Terry McAweeney, Mark Polizzotti, and Emiko K. Usui.

For helping the MFA explore the viability of this exhibition in its early stages, we thank local car enthusiast and MFA supporter Langdon Wheeler. Mr. Wheeler graciously introduced us to Paul Russell, one of the world's preeminent restorers of vintage automobiles, who has meticulously revital- ized a number of Mr. Lauren's cars. Mr. Russell served as a consultant for the exhibition in a multitude of ways, from supplying technical and historical data to advising about the practical issues of displaying cars in a museum. Added thanks should go to Janet Oliver of Mr. Russell's staff for how she ably oversaw many of the day-to-day details of those same activities. We are also grateful to Mark Reinwald, curator of the Ralph Lauren collection, for his help with several vital tasks, especially the transport of numerous cars to and from a photo studio.

From the Larz Anderson Auto Museum in Brookline, Massachusetts, director John Sweeney and curator Evan Ide have been supportive of this exhibition in many ways, and it has been a pleasure to work with them. Various car collectors and scholars provided essential contacts in our search for period photography and other graphic material for both this book and the actual exhibition. Included here are Miles Collier, Leslie Kendall, and Charles Levy.

The sumptuous photos of Michael Furman and Martyn Goddard speak for themselves, and we thank them for lending their artistic eyes to this book. And finally, our appreciation goes to the book's two authors, Beverly Rae Kimes and Winston Goodfellow for bringing alive the stories behind these wonderful cars.

DARCY KURONEN, Curator

CREDITS

MFA PUBLICATIONS
a division of the Museum of Fine Arts, Boston
465 Huntington Avenue
Boston, Massachusetts 02115
www.mfa-publications.org

Published in conjunction with the exhibition
"Speed, Style, and Beauty: Cars from the Ralph Lauren Collection,"
organized by the Museum of Fine Arts, Boston, from March 6 to July 3, 2005.

Generous support for the exhibition was provided by **Merrill Lynch**

For a complete listing of MFA Publications, please contact the publisher
at the above address, or call 617 369 3438.

COVER: 1938 Bugatti Type 57SC Atlantic Coupe (see pp. 64–71); photograph © Michael Furman

ISBN 0-87846-685-1 (hardcover) · ISBN 0-87846-687-8 (softcover)
Library of Congress Control Number: 2004115071

Available through D.A.P. / Distributed Art Publishers
155 Sixth Avenue, 2nd floor, New York, New York 10013
Tel.: 212 627 1999 · Fax: 212 627 9484

Manuscript edited by Mark Polizzotti and Emiko K. Usui
Copyedited and proofread by Denise Bergman and Julia Gaviria
Typeset in Filosofia by Fran Presti-Fazio
Production by Terry McAweeney
Text and cover design by Susan Marsh
Printed on acid-free paper
Printed and bound by Mondadori Printing, Italy

FOURTH PRINTING